Arbour   Ottawa Valley's Environmental Shoppe
800 Bank Street, In the Glebe, Ottawa
K1S 3V8   (613) 567-3168

Honey Lip Balm Recipe

1 ounce bar beeswax   *3 TBSP APPROX.*
1/2 cup sweet almond oil (or other veg. oil)
1 tsp. honey

Optional ingredients:
1 tsp. flavour (vanilla extract, peppermint oil etc.)
1 vitamin E capsule (pierced)

In a sauce pan over low heat warm the veg. oil and
melt the beeswax into it. Take off the heat and add
the other ingredients. Blend and pour immediately
into the lip balm jars (small jam jars work very well).

Note: Consistency may vary with geographic areas.
If the lip balm is too hard, rewarm and add more
sweet almond oil. If it is too soft, add more beeswax.
It's really easy!

For a more healing balm you may then add powdered
golden seal, comfrey, calendula, or natural essence oils
depending upon the result you wish to achieve. Enjoy !

handmade soap

recipes for crafting soap at home

Country Living

handmade soap

recipes for crafting soap at home

text by Mike Hulbert

photography by Keith Scott Morton

styled by Christine Churchill

foreword by Rachel Newman

HEARST BOOKS NEW YORK

Recognizing the importance of preserving what has been written, it
is the policy of William Morrow and Company, Inc., and its imprints
and affiliates to have the books it publishes printed on acid-free
paper, and we exert our best efforts to that end.

Library of Congress Cataloging-in-Publication Data
Hulbert, Michael.
Coutry living handmade soap : recipes for crafting soap at home /
    text by Michael Hulbert : photography by Keith Scott Morton ;
    foreword by Rachel Newman. — 1st U.S. ed.
            p.   cm.
    Includes index.
    ISBN 0-688-15562-6
    1. Soap.   I. Country living (New York, N.Y.) II. Title.
TP991.H86   1998
668' .124—dc21   97-41040
                                                       CIP

Printed in Singapore
First U.S. Edition
1 2 3 4 5 6 7 8 9 10

Text set in Galliard

Art Director: Patti Ratchford
Designer: Gretchen Mergenthaler
Editor: Camilla Crichton

Produced by Smallwood and Stewart, Inc., New York City

table of contents

foreword

There is nothing quite so inviting as the look of handmade soap, sitting in a pretty basket in the bathroom, perched on a kitchen counter, or wrapped in bright ribbon for gift giving. We at *Country Living* magazine have long been fans of homemade soaps, admiring them for their integrity and purity. When you make your own soap, you know exactly what is going into it and, therefore, can avoid harsh irritants and include only the finest of ingredients. As interest in aromatherapy, herbs, and natural products has increased in recent years, we felt that a book on soap-making, a gratifying and practical pastime, was timely.

Soap-making offers an amazing array of end products—luxurious perfumed soaps for the body, practical soaps for cleaning your home, soaps for face and hair that are specially tailored for you and your loved ones—the possibilities are endless. You can experiment with combinations of ingredients, colors, herbs, essential oils, and shapes, to come up with a soap that is perfect for giving, or a sensuous indulgence for yourself. Soaps also provide wonderful decorative accents for your home when placed strategically in a room to imbue it with aroma and color.

Whether you are an experienced soap-maker or are simply intrigued by the creative possibilities of making soap, we at *Country Living* hope this book inspires and encourages you to experience the joy of creating something practical and beautiful for yourself, your home, and your family.

—Rachel Newman, Editor-in-Chief

introduction

We've been making soap on our farm in North Carolina since the late 1970s. What started out as my wife's hobby, utilizing her knowledge of herbs and their therapeutic properties, soon became a passion—now it's a way of life as well as our livelihood in the guise of Creation Herbal Products. In this book, we share our enjoyment of handmade soap and what we've learned during the past twenty years.

Making soap is not a difficult process—no more challenging than following a recipe for pastry and turning it into a pie. Soap is made up of three basic ingredients: water, lye, and fats (oils). When a lye-and-water solution is mixed with fats, a reaction takes place between the hydrogen, oxygen, sodium, and fatty acid molecules. This is called saponification, and the end result is a substance that is made up of five parts soap and one part glycerin. Glycerin—a rich emollient prized for its ability to soften the skin—is retained in handmade soap but in commercial soap it is extracted, leaving behind the hard, drying bars of soap we purchase in stores and supermarkets.

No one really knows how soap-making began, but according to an ancient Roman legend, the very first soaps were created quite by accident, on a hill not far from Rome known as Mount Sapo (from which the term saponification is derived). On the hill stood a temple where animals were sacrificed in burnt offerings to the Roman divinities. Below ran the river Tiber, where womenfolk brought their bundles of laundry and washed them in the gently flowing river water. It didn't take the women very long to realize that the best time to take clothes to the riverbank was after it rained—somehow the water seemed softer and more cleansing, and the laundry easier to do. Soon, the connection was made—the white chunks clinging to the rocks on the hill were providing the cleansing magic.

What occurred when the rain fell is very simple: a crude type of lye solution was being leached from the wood ashes on the temple altar. The solution combined with the unburned animal fats as it trickled down the hillside, eventually drying and solidifying—creating a very simple form of soap.

In the centuries of experimentation that followed its initial discovery, soap-making slowly evolved into the sophisticated industry we know today. In eighteenth-century America, for example, soap-making was still a household chore. In those days wood ashes were collected and mixed with rainwater. On soap-making day the resultant lye solution was mixed with molten tallow (animal fat), which had also been rendered in the home. Eventually "soap chandlers" appeared—they bought fat from homesteaders, rendered it into tallow, made soap, and then sold it back to the homesteaders. They were the forerunners of modern soap manufacturers.

Today, commercial soap is manufactured in a process known as the "continuous method" and, as the name suggests, the soap is produced in vast containers where the ingredients are continuously added at one end of the vat while soap is continuously removed from the other. During the process, glycerin is removed.

For the most part, these commercially produced soaps do their job. They get you clean, although they lather meagerly, have a synthetic fragrance, and leave your skin feeling dry and a little like sandpaper. Handmade soap, on the other hand, lathers richly, is naturally fragrant, and moisturizes as well as cleanses, leaving your skin feeling clean, soft, and supple. Handmade soap is also innately reassuring—full of character, natural goodness, and beneficial ingredients such as essential oils and herbs.

The soap-making processes described in this book are divided into three categories: cold-process, hand-milling, and melt-and-pour. The cold-process method is the one that most closely resembles the soap-making techniques of yesteryear: a lye solution is combined with various oils and poured into molds to harden. To make hand-milled soap, cold-process soap is grated, melted, and remolded, which produces a harder, longer-lasting bar, with a smoother and more consistent texture than the original cold-process soap. Lastly, the melt-and-pour method, which is the simplest technique, involves melting down a block of glycerin and pouring it into molds to harden.

In all three of these soap-making processes, special ingredients—oils, goat's milk, beeswax, rosewater, flower petals, spices, oats, cornmeal—are added to give the resulting soaps their individuality and the special characteristics for which they are valued.

Unless otherwise stated, the recipes in this book will yield forty ounces of soap. Always be sure to wear the suggested protective clothing, and it is also essential that you read and thoroughly understand all the information in Chapter One before attempting any of the Basic Recipes or the recipes in the succeeding chapters.

chapter one **the**

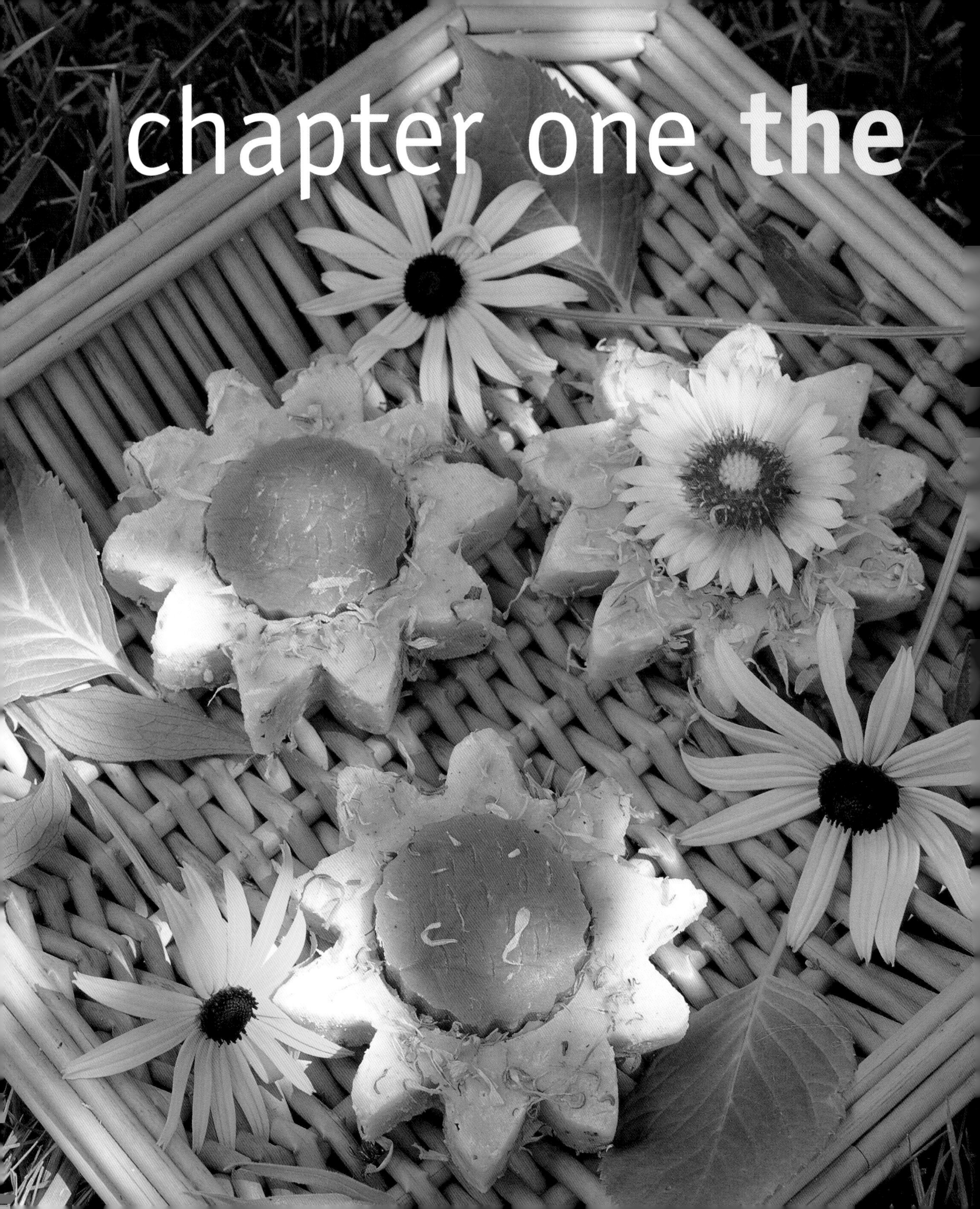

basic recipes

You are at the start of an odyssey: soap-making is one of the most exciting and satisfying crafts—and completely addictive. In the beginning, the results of your endeavors may not always be what you were expecting—perfection takes practice after all. But, if you like to create, and enjoy puttering around the kitchen, you will adore making soap and will soon become adept.

In this chapter, the three soap-making methods—cold-process, hand-milling, and melt-and-pour—are described in step-by-step detail. Read this chapter carefully before you begin making soap—it contains important advice about handling lye, and it is essential that you understand the various processes.

The seven Basic Recipes for making cold-process soaps are also included in this chapter. These are the building-blocks for your future as a soap-maker. Each of the recipes can be endlessly adapted to create new recipes for soaps to suit your requirements. Indeed, each of the cold-process and hand-milling recipes in the following chapters of this book are based on these seven Basic Recipes.

The first part of this chapter lists the basic ingredients and equipment you need to gather before embarking on your soap-making adventure.

ingredients

When you begin looking for the ingredients you need for making soap, the places to start are your local grocery store or food co-op, natural food stores, Asian food markets, and in your garden.

Failing that, the resources section (see page 108) of this book lists suppliers who will have everything you'll need, in quantities small and inexpensive enough to make soap-making practical. Of course, when you become more ambitious, they also sell ingredients in larger quantities too!

lye—chemically called sodium hydroxide, lye is also known as caustic soda and is readily available on your grocer's shelf. Domestically, it is most commonly used as a drain cleaner and comes in bead, granular, and flake form. The best-known brand in the United States is Red Devil™, which is packaged in twelve-ounce containers. Don't use other brands unless you can get confirmation from the manufacturer that they are pure sodium hydroxide, because they often contain heavy metals and other ingredients which may be hazardous to your skin. Handle lye with care; it is volatile and can be dangerous, especially when wet. Carefully read the safety section on page 22 and the warnings on the lye container.

water—lye is diluted in water to make up the solution which will be mixed with the oils. It is important that the water is tepid (room temperature, between 65°F and 75°F) because combining lye with water that is too hot can cause a volcanic eruption, which is potentially dangerous, but also difficult to clean up. On the other hand, if the water is too cool, the solution may not reach the temperature needed for some recipes.

Distilled water is recommended but not essential; just be aware that if you use ordinary tap water, a layer of scum may form on top of the lye solution. This scum is a result of minerals and impurities in the water. Before you combine the solution with the oils, skim off and discard the scum.

oils—many different kinds of oils or fats can be used for making soap. They each have their own set of properties, so they are usually used in combination.

Pressed from the huge beans of the castor plant, castor oil is primarily used to enrich soap and make it more emollient and moisturizing. (An emollient softens the skin.) Castor oil is also often added to shampoo, because the small bubbles it produces gives the lather intensity.

Refined from the meat of the coconut, coconut oil has long been a common ingredient in soap and candle-making. Coconut oil enhances soap hardness and produces a creamy lather, but it has a tendency to dry the skin, so it is generally used in combination with other, more emollient, oils that offset its drying qualities. Coconut oil is not usually readily available in grocery stores—although you may find it in good health food stores and Asian food markets—but it can be purchased from several of the companies listed in the resources section.

Refined from the jojoba bush, a native of the western United States, jojoba oil is very rich, moisturizing, and conditioning, which makes it a good addition to any shampoo or moisturizing soap recipe. Always request the deodorized variety from your supplier, otherwise you'll find that jojoba oil has an unpleasant odor that you won't want in your finished soaps. Jojoba oil is not widely available, so you'll need to consult the resources section.

There are many kinds of olive oil commonly available for making soap. Naturally pressed extra-virgin and virgin olive oils are widely available, but while they will work in soap-making they are usually expensive and tend to make the soap smell faintly of olives. Many soap-makers therefore prefer to use pomace olive oil. Pomace is the oil extracted from the very last pressing of the olives and produces odorless soaps which cure into very hard, long-lasting bars. Olive oil in general produces a very mild, non-drying soap with a creamy lather.

Palm oils are refined from palm trees, including the trunks and leaves, and the tree's large seeds. Some palm oils can be found in Asian food markets, but because these oils tend to be less refined they often have an orange hue. (To a certain degree, however, this can be used to affect the final color of soap.) More commonly available from suppliers are the white refined versions of the oil (see page 108). Palm oil makes for a mild soap with a long-lasting lather and enhances the final hardness of the bar. Like coconut oil, however, palm oil tends to be drying, so keep the total palm content under twenty percent of the total oils in a recipe.

Nature's richest source of vitamin E, wheat germ oil is excellent for enriching recipes. The oil gives a luxurious creaminess to the lather and adds moisture, which inhibits the lather from drying the skin. Wheat germ oil is readily available in natural food stores, but make sure you buy cold-pressed wheat germ oil—not unrefined or cold-processed wheat germ oil, which may contain unsafe solvent residues.

A rich, white, creamy emollient, cocoa butter adds soothing and moisturizing characteristics to soaps without affecting their color. Chocolate lovers beware, however: the aroma of cocoa butter can be enticing before saponification takes place. Cocoa butter is available at health food stores, good pharmacies, and candy-making supply stores, as well as through the suppliers listed in the resources section.

Although tallow can be rendered from any animal fat, the recipes in this book refer to tallow rendered from beef fat. Although vegetarians would prefer that soap-makers never use it, tallow does produce a hard soap with a wonderfully rich lather, and it is also a very traditional ingredient.

You can easily render your own tallow. Purchase beef fat from your local butcher or supermarket. Put the fat into a crock pot or large roasting pan and cover with water. Cover and bake in a 200°F oven for at least twelve hours or overnight, then allow to cool. Once it is cold, pour off the water, and rinse. The resulting tallow will be pearly white and ready to use. (To render sufficient tallow for Basic Recipe Six, use eight pounds beef fat and eight quarts water.) Supermarket meat departments and butcher shops will often give you beef fat free of charge or sell it to you for only a few cents per pound, which makes it one of the

least expensive soap-making ingredients. Rendered tallow is available commercially from some soap-making suppliers, if you prefer (see the resources section).

other ingredients— once the primary ingredients—the lye solution and the oils—have been blended, all sorts of secondary ingredients can be added to enhance the basic soap.

Add goat's milk to your soap instead of water when you want to create an especially mild and gentle soap. Goat's milk will add a creamy richness to the lather and is very emollient. To prevent spoiling, store goat's milk soap in a warm dry place with good ventilation so it will dry quickly—thus avoiding the possibility of the soap developing mold before it is cured. (Mold is no longer a concern once the soap is fully cured.)

Wonderfully emollient—moistening and protecting the skin—glycerin occurs naturally in vegetable and animal fats. It is also the by-product of the cold-process reaction and is extracted from commercial soaps. You can buy glycerin soap-base for making melt-and-pour soaps at craft stores, where it usually comes in one-pound bags or blocks. Liquid glycerin, which is used in cold-process soaps, is also available at craft stores. Both types can also be bought via mail order through one of the suppliers listed in the resources section.

Fragrant essential oils are distilled from the leaves, flowers, berries, barks, and roots of various herbs and shrubs. Most are antiseptic, antibiotic, antifungal, and antiviral to varying degrees. They are used in soap-making for their scents, but also for their therapeutic and medicinal qualities.

Essential oils are highly concentrated, and some are extremely toxic if used improperly—all the quantities listed in this book are safe, however. Information about essential oils is readily available, and you should consult an appropriate reference book or an herbalist before using new essential oils for the first time.

Most of the recipes in this book include some kind of botanical—fresh and dried herbs and spices, abrasives such as cornmeal and oats, etc.

equipment

To begin your soap-making adventure, you need to gather the following basic equipment—most of which can be found in your kitchen. Once you've made a few batches of soap, you'll probably adapt this list to suit your own needs, and then go on to develop all sorts of novel and imaginative adaptations for other unsuspecting household items.

Keep in mind that once you've used kitchen equipment for making soap, you must keep them separate from other kitchen utensils and use them only for soap—never again for preparing food.

Lye reacts with aluminum, tin, zinc, and most other metals, so when you are selecting containers in which to store and mix lye, make sure they are glass, enamel, plastic, stainless steel, or oven-proof stoneware. (Even though stainless steel doesn't react with lye immediately, wash any stainless-steel utensils as soon as possible after exposure or they will begin to corrode.)

To make soap successfully, an accurate scale is needed. The reaction between the lye solution and the oils is directly affected by their weight—if they are weighed incorrectly, saponification won't occur. Look for a scale that weighs tenths of ounces, which an ordinary kitchen scale normally can't do. An electronic digital scale is best, primarily because it's easier to read! Good scales aren't hard to find, but some suppliers are nevertheless listed in the resources section.

Accurately measuring the primary ingredients (lye solution and the oils) is critical to the success of the end product. That's not the case, however, when it comes to the additives: essential oils, spices, botanicals, and the like. Nevertheless, use measuring cups & spoons to give you a rough idea of how much you added—or you'll never remember what you did when you want to re-create an extra-special soap.

You need a lye-resistant container that holds at least two cups, for measuring out the lye.

For mixing the lye-and-water solution, you need to have another container, also lye-resistant, which will hold at least eight cups. Select a container with a wide opening, such as a beverage pitcher, so it will be easy to pour and skim off any scum.

A pouring jug, also lye-resistant and with an eight-cup capacity, is needed for pouring the lye solution into the oils. It works best if you use an ordinary glass jar for this. Modify the lid by piercing two holes—one for air and the other for pouring. With this jar, you can use one hand to pour the lye solution in a slow, steady stream into the oils, while stirring with the other.

For melting and mixing the oils, use a stainless-steel mixing pot or other lye-resistant and heat-proof container. You'll also use this pot for blending the lye solution into the oils, so it must hold twelve cups liquid.

A pair of thermometers, such as stainless-steel meat thermometers, is necessary for measuring the temperature of the lye solution and the oils. Select thermometers that will allow you to measure temperatures between 70°F and 200°F and which will give you an accurate response quickly. Some thermometers take three to four minutes to give a good reading—a thermometer that gives a correct reading within a few seconds is preferable.

Two water baths are needed—one to cool the lye solution (so it must be large enough to hold the solution's container) and one to heat or cool the oils (so it must be large enough to hold the mixing pot). A bucket, a large basin or bowl, or any other generously sized container would be ideal.

Stainless-steel, sturdy plastic, or wooden spoons for stirring—keep three or four handy, since they have a tendency to vanish just when you need them!

A lye-resistant pouring pitcher—most heavy-duty plastic pitchers will do well for pouring newly made soap into the molds.

Find yourself a rubber spatula so that you can scrape every last drop of that precious soap out of the pouring pitcher and into the molds.

There are many different molds you can use for molding your soap. You can either pour the liquid soap into a single large mold, and slice the resulting block into bars once it's dried, or into individual molds. It's not until you start looking that you realize your home is full of soap molds masquerading as something else—as plastic ice-cream containers or microwave dishes, for example. Cardboard shoe and shirt boxes are also disguised soap molds (but these need to be lined with plastic wrap before you fill them with soap). Just about any plastic container could be suitable for use as a soap mold: drawer organizers work very well and are available in a large variety of shapes and sizes, sections of PVC pipe (use pipe ends for making perfect shaving mug refills), and ice-cube trays, which make good molds for tiny guest soaps. Improvised soap molds aren't hard to find, but more specialized soap molds are, and are usually expensive. It's well worth looking in good craft stores for candle molds; so long as the mold is plastic and the opening at the top is wider than the rest of the mold, they'll work fine and you may come up with some interesting shapes. Also readily available at craft stores are plastic sheets stamped with impressions of themed shapes: seashells, geometrics, and so forth. These make attractive soaps and are especially good for melt-and-pour soaps. Finally, the resources section lists some suppliers of molds. When you're hunting for molds, remember that all the recipes in this book, unless otherwise specified, make forty ounces of soap (twenty 2-ounce bars, or ten 4-ounce bars).

You should collect an assortment of pot holders, oven mitts, and cotton rags for holding and resting hot containers.

A food processor and/or a spice grinder will also be useful. While this is not immediately necessary, such equipment will prove endlessly useful for chopping and grinding fresh and dried botanicals.

You'll also need strainers and cheesecloth for straining infusions, extracts, and other herbal concoctions.

Finally, you will need old blankets and pieces of cardboard for insulating your soaps while they set.

safety in the soap kitchen

As long as you handle lye with respect, soap-making is a completely safe process. Lye is a poison: it is fatal if swallowed, its fumes are toxic, and it will burn most surfaces it comes into contact with, including your skin.

The first rule of safe soap-making is to wear eye protectors: so make putting on goggles the first step in any procedure involving lye, lye solution, or fresh soap, and you are well on your way to making soap safely. Be very careful about touching your face and eyes while making soap. An almost invisible amount of lye or lye solution (even the vapors) can cause great discomfort and could damage your eyes. If you sense the slightest discomfort or burning in your eyes, stop what you're doing and immediately flush them with running water.

The second rule is to wear a face mask—the disposable kind that construction workers use is ideal. You can buy these masks, along with safety glasses or goggles, at your local hardware store. Always wear a face mask during the lye-and-water blending process, since the fumes are noxious and should not be breathed directly; but you are strongly advised to wear your mask during all the stages of making cold-process soap. Because of the lye-fumes, it is also important to make soap in a well-ventilated area.

Thirdly, always wear rubber gloves. These will protect your hands and lower arms—the parts of your body most likely to be splashed. If lye, lye solution, or fresh soap come into contact with your skin, it may only irritate, but it could cause a severe burn. At first your skin will feel slippery, then it will start to itch, and finally begin to burn. Immediately apply vinegar (the acid will neutralize the lye) to the affected area, and then rinse with water.

So, the fourth rule of safe soap-making is to keep a jar of vinegar handy at all times when you are making soap. A half-gallon plastic jug of white vinegar kept within easy reach is ideal.

Finally, take care of the lye. When you open a container of lye, it immediately begins to absorb water from the atmosphere: this weakens its strength and causes it to clump up in the container, making it difficult to work with. Only open the container to weigh out enough lye for the batch of soap you are working on; then immediately seal the container. If you spill any lye, lye solution, or fresh soap, immediately wash the area with water and detergent, rinse with clean water, and then wipe dry.

the cold-process method

Making soap by the cold-process method is actually very straightforward. In a nutshell, you mix the water and the lye, and then use a water bath to bring down the solution's temperature. Next you melt and mix the oils, and use another water bath to bring the oils' temperature up or down. The objective is to match the temperatures of the solution and oils so they can be mixed together. This is the most difficult part of the method; however once you've had a bit of practice, you will soon become adept.

The first few times you make soap, carefully follow the method below. Then, after you have become familiar with the cold-process method, and are beginning to feel confident with the procedure, you can alter the order in which you take the following steps to suit your particular method of heating and cooling the lye solution and oils. Whether you start by making the lye solution or melting the oils is not really significant.

Always protect your eyes with goggles when making soap.

Wear a face mask when mixing and handling the lye solution.

Put on rubber gloves before you begin.

Keep a jar of vinegar handy.

Do not open your lye container until you are ready to use it; immediately close the container after use.

Only make soap where you have access to running water.

Store your soap-making equipment and freshly made soaps in a safe place, away from kitchen utensils, children, and pets.

1 First, make sure that you have a few hours during which you will not be disturbed, especially by children or pets—most of the recipes in this book will involve two to three hours of your undivided attention.

2 Put on some old, comfortable clothes (that won't matter if they are damaged), and prepare your work area. Unless you are using a space you have dedicated solely to soap-making, protect your work surfaces and floors against spills with newspaper (and keep some extra paper handy). Assemble all of your equipment and prepare the ingredients and molds. Unless otherwise specified, all of the recipes in this book make forty ounces soap. Make sure you set out molds with sufficient

capacity for the entire batch of soap. You can do this by filling the molds with water, then weighing the water to check there is forty ounces. You will also need to line any molds that are not made of plastic with plastic wrap.

3 Finally, put on your goggles, face mask, and rubber gloves. Now you're ready to begin.

4 Start by preparing the lye solution. Place the container you are going to use for mixing the solution on your scale, and reset it to zero. Measure the required amount of tepid water (65°F to 75°F) and remove the pot from the scale. Then weigh the lye into its separate container in the same way.

While stirring the water, slowly pour in the lye. Take care here—the chemical reaction that is triggered as the lye dissolves in the water will cause the solution to become extremely hot. It won't look as if it's boiling, but the actual temperature will be 5°F to10°F higher than the boiling temperature of water (212°F). The solution will also turn cloudy.

Remembering not to breathe the fumes directly, continue stirring until the lye is thoroughly dissolved—a couple of minutes should be enough—then check the temperature of the solution with one of your thermometers. Always be sure the thermometer doesn't touch the bottom or side of the container, which would give a false reading. Using a cold water bath, bring the lye solution down to the temperature specified in the recipe.

5 Now blend the oils. Place the pot that you are going to use for melting the oils (and mixing the soap) on your scale and reset it to zero. Weigh the solid oils and then melt them over medium heat. While they melt, place another container on the scale, set it to zero, and weigh the liquid oils.

When the solid oils have completely melted, stir in the liquid oils and check the temperature with your other thermometer—again, don't allow it to touch the bottom or side of the container. Using a water bath, either heat or cool the oils to the desired temperature for blending. Try not to overheat the oils or you will waste valuable time waiting for them to cool.

6 The objective now is to match the temperature of the lye solution with the temperature of the oils, to the temperature specified in the recipe. Check both temperatures every few minutes and use the water baths to bring down, bring up, or maintain the temperatures.

This procedure is a little tricky, but matching the temperatures will get easier as you become more experienced. It helps if you remember that it takes the lye solution longer to cool than it takes the oils—so if the oils are too hot, the lye solution will be too cold by

While it is possible to pour the lye solution from the same container you mixed it in, it is easier to use a pouring jar—this means that you don't add too much lye solution too quickly, which would greatly increase the stirring time. Using a pouring jar allows you to start the saponification reaction in a slower but more intense fashion as the water, lye, and oil molecules start a chain reaction that increases as you trickle the lye solution into the oils. Adding the lye solution too quickly can also cause your batch to curdle or separate (see opposite page).

the time the oils have cooled. In this case set your lye solution in a hot water bath to keep it warm while the oils cool to the desired range. When the temperatures match, carefully transfer the lye solution to the pouring jar.

7 It is now time to begin the saponification process. Slowly drizzle the lye solution into the oils, while constantly stirring. Stir the mixture quite quickly and with intent, making sure that you reach every part of the container.

Continue stirring until you have blended all of the lye solution into the oils.

8 After combining the lye solution with the oil, you need to keep stirring while the mixture saponifies. When the reaction is nearing completion it will begin to "trace" (thicken). The soap has traced when a drizzle from the mixing

spoon retains its shape for a few seconds on the surface of the soap. Tracing sometimes takes some time to occur. If, after you have stirred for fifteen minutes, your soap has not traced, take a rest for ten minutes, checking every few minutes in case the soap has altered. After ten minutes is up, begin stirring again for another fifteen minutes, and then take another rest. Continue in this manner until the soap traces. Your soaps should usually trace within the first half hour, but it can sometimes take as long as one or two hours.

9 As soon as the soap has traced, add your essential oils, herbs, and any other ingredients, stirring until they are well blended. Work quickly now—the soap will continue to thicken and may become too thick to pour.

10 Once the new ingredients are well blended, you are ready to pour the soap into the molds. If you are pouring into individual molds, you will need to transfer the soap to your pouring pitcher. But if you are using a large single mold, go right ahead and pour directly into the mold. Use your rubber spatula to scrape every valuable ounce of the soap from the side of the mixing pot and into the mold.

11 Cover the newly poured soap with cardboard and old blankets so it doesn't cool too rapidly. It will take anywhere from a few hours to a couple of days for the soap to harden enough to unmold—individual recipes will guide you in this. As a general rule, however, the soap is set and ready to unmold when it is solid and feels firm to the touch.

12 For unmolding, protect your hands with rubber gloves or disposable latex gloves, which are ideal because they are thinner and you can feel the soap more easily. The soap will still be quite soft and so, once unmolded, stack or lay it out to cure in a warm well-ventilated area. At this point, you can also cut large blocks of soap into bars—or cure the block as it is, and slice it up later. All of the recipes in this book include a curing period. This is the time during which the soap will dry into hard bars. During this time, the pH level of the soap will also decrease to the safe zone—when you can use the soap on your skin. (When the soap is poured it is still highly alkaline.)

trouble shooting

So long as you understand the cold-process method and follow it to the letter, at least to begin with, you shouldn't have any problems. But occasionally difficulties do occur and the most common ones are listed below. Not all of them are disastrous and rest assured that even the most experienced soap-makers sometimes encounter them. They are usually caused by improperly stored lye, inaccurate weighing, and blending at the wrong temperature. curdling—this occasionally occurs during stirring, while waiting for the soap to trace. The soap mixture begins to resemble cottage cheese. This is most often caused by miscalculations when weighing the lye or oils, so check your scales. It can also be caused by mixing the lye solution into the oils at too high a temperature. If curdling happens, your batch has failed—you should discard it and try again. no trace—sometimes a batch of soap just won't trace. If a soap won't trace but it does become somewhat thick, add your essential oils and herbs and pour it in the mold anyway, it will probably be fine. If, however, the soap remains thin and watery, it could be an indication that your lye is no good: improperly stored lye will not be strong enough to saponify the oils. If your lye is in question, discard it and begin again with fresh lye.

soap seizure—essential oils occasionally affect tracing with dramatic results. Upon adding the essential oil the soap mixture may suddenly solidify—becoming very hot and very hard, very quickly. So quickly in fact, that the mixing spoon may become stuck in the hard soap and have to be cut out with a knife. This is an extreme example, but it's worth remembering when you set out your molds. If you're planning to pour into individual molds, put out a single mold large enough to hold the whole batch of soap, in case you have to bail out and go for a big block of soap at the last minute. Happily the soap is usually fine.

separation—soap sometimes separates in the mold—this appears as a layer of oil on the surface of the soap. Do not touch! When separation occurs, it is an indication that the soap has not saponified; and so the lye is still active. Occasionally, it is possible to rescue the soap by stirring it right in the mold. But if it separates again, the batch has failed, and you should discard it and try again. Separation is usually caused by incorrectly weighing the lye or the oils, or by blending at too high a temperature.

soda ash—soaps occasionally develop this problem, which happens when sodium carbonate is formed by the reaction of carbon dioxide in the air with lye on the surface of the newly poured soap. Soda ash appears as a thin white layer of powdery crystals on the outside of the soap. Covering your soaps immediately after pouring, so that they're not exposed to the air, helps to prevent this. If it does occur, however, it can usually be scraped away with a paring knife or wiped off with a dampened cloth.

creating a soap kitchen

If you have the space, it's worth creating a place dedicated to soap-making. When you're starting out, your kitchen will do: just be sure your floors and work surfaces are protected with newspaper. Whatever you do, don't choose your beautifully refinished oak table in the dining room for mixing soap! A separate soap-making area should have a sink that drains well and that has hot and cold running water. You will also need a hot plate for melting oils—a UL-approved hot plate on a work table is more than adequate. Your basement or garage are probably ideal places; just make sure that they are well ventilated.

basic recipe one

A mild, off-white Castille-type soap, this soap cures into nice, hard bars that produce lots of exploding lather. It is an excellent all-purpose soap and a good choice for hand-milling recipes because it is so versatile: you can remold this recipe into both body bars (see Chapter Two) and soaps for domestic use (see Chapter Three).

1. Prepare the mold.

2. Blend the water and lye. Set aside and cool to 100°F.

3. Melt the coconut and palm oils. Blend in the olive oil and either heat or cool to 100°F.

4. Once the temperatures match, blend the lye solution into the oils.

5. Stir the mixture until the soap traces. At trace, pour into the prepared mold.

6. Leave the soap to set for 4 to 8 hours, or until the soap is solid and firm to the touch. Release the soap from the mold and allow to cure for 6 to 8 weeks.

14 ounces tepid water

6 ounces lye

12 ounces coconut oil

8 ounces palm oil

20 ounces olive oil

basic recipe two

Excellent for sensitive skins, this recipe can be adapted into wonderful moisturizing soaps, shaving soaps, and baby soaps. The recipe produces a mild, creamy, light yellow soap that yields a foamy, shampoo-type lather. This is a good candidate for hand-milling recipes where emollient oils and soothing herbs will be added.

1. Prepare the mold.

2. Blend the water and lye. Set aside and cool to 100°F.

3. Melt the coconut and palm oils. Blend in the castor, olive, and wheat germ oils and either heat or cool to 100°F.

4. Once the temperatures match, blend the lye solution into the oils.

5. Stir the mixture until the soap traces. At trace, pour into the prepared mold.

6. Leave the soap to set for 8 to 14 hours, or until the soap is solid and firm to the touch. Release the soap from the mold and allow to cure for 2 to 4 weeks.

14 ounces tepid water

5.9 ounces lye

12 ounces coconut oil

6 ounces palm oil

10 ounces castor oil

8 ounces olive oil

4 ounces wheat germ oil

basic recipe three

This recipe makes a very white, hard soap which immediately produces large exploding bubbles in the lather. It is excellent for both normal and oily skin and for developing into spicy hand-milled soaps. This soap also works well in recipes that include abrasives and for domestic soap recipes (see Chapter Three).

1. Prepare the mold.

2. Blend the water and lye. Set aside and cool to 110°F.

3. Melt the coconut and palm oils. Blend in the olive oil and either heat or cool to 110°F.

4. Once the temperatures match, blend the lye solution into the oils.

5. Stir the mixture until the soap traces. At trace, pour into the prepared mold.

6. Leave the soap to set for 3 to 6 hours, or until the soap is solid and firm to the touch. Release the soap from the mold and allow to cure for 4 to 6 weeks.

15 ounces tepid water

6.3 ounces lye

20 ounces coconut oil

6 ounces palm oil

14 ounces olive oil

basic recipe four

A large amount of olive oil and the addition of beeswax make this Castille-type soap, which is the color of buttercream, mild and long-lasting. This soap produces a delicate lather, which readily becomes rich and creamy when it is worked up. It is an excellent soap for sensitive skins, and because the soap cures into hard bars, it is a wonderful choice for hand-milling recipes.

1. Prepare the mold.

2. Blend the water and lye. Set aside and cool to 150°F.

3. Melt the beeswax and the coconut and palm oils. Blend in the olive oil and either heat or cool to 150°F.

4. Once the temperatures match, blend the lye solution into the oils.

5. Stir the mixture until the soap traces. At trace, pour into the prepared mold.

6. Leave the soap to set for 6 to 12 hours, or until the soap is solid and firm to the touch. Release the soap from the mold and allow to cure for 4 to 6 weeks.

14 ounces tepid water

5 ounces lye

6 ounces beeswax

4 ounces coconut oil

2 ounces palm oil

28 ounces olive oil

basic recipe *five*

This recipe produces a very versatile and extremely gentle, off-white soap with long-lasting bubbles. The lye is mixed with goat's milk instead of water, which means you need to watch the solution carefully. First it will be cloudy, then it will turn light brown, before finally becoming orange. The trick is to blend the oils before you dissolve the lye—because you need to mix the lye solution into the oils before the solution turns orange.

1. Prepare the mold.

2. Melt the coconut and palm oils. Blend in the olive oil and either heat or cool to 120°F.

3. Blend the goat's milk and lye. Stir to dissolve the lye.

4. Blend the lye solution into the oils when the solution is light brown.

5. Stir the mixture until the soap traces. At trace, pour into the prepared mold.

6. Leave the soap to set for 12 to 24 hours, or until the soap is solid and firm to the touch. Release the soap from the mold and allow to cure for 6 to 8 weeks.

12 ounces coconut oil

4 ounces palm oil

24 ounces olive oil

16 ounces tepid goat's milk

5.9 ounces lye

basic recipe six

The use of beef tallow in this recipe produces a classic pioneer-style soap—long-lasting with a mild creamy lather, it lent itself to many uses around the farm in the old days. The soap is sometimes a little grainy in texture—the results depend upon the consistency of the tallow from batch to batch. The soap traces readily and dries easily, producing hard bars when fully cured.

1. Prepare the mold.

2. Blend the water and lye. Set aside and cool to 120°F.

3. Melt the tallow and either heat or cool to 120°F.

4. Once the temperatures match, blend the lye solution into the tallow.

5. Stir the mixture until the soap traces. At trace, pour into the prepared mold.

6. Leave the soap to set for 2 to 6 hours, or until the soap is solid and firm to the touch. Release the soap from the mold and allow to cure for 4 to 6 weeks.

16 ounces tepid water

5.4 ounces lye

2.5 pounds beef tallow

basic recipe seven
pure castille

Castille, a classic soap, comes from the Mediterranean area, where the abundance of olive oil prompted its development in the Middle Ages. This is a soap for the diligent stirrer because it sometimes takes a while to trace; just keep going—so long as your lye is good, it will eventually trace. (It may take a day or two to occur, but you can leave it unattended for long periods; even overnight.) Long-lasting with creamy bubbles, choose this soap for hand-milling into gentle herb and baby soaps. Don't worry if Castille soap develops yellow spots during curing—they are characteristic of the soap.

1. Prepare the mold.

2. Blend the water and lye. Set aside and cool to 120°F.

3. Heat the olive oil to 120°F.

4. Once the temperatures match, blend the lye solution into the oil.

5. Stir the mixture until the soap traces. At trace, pour into the prepared mold.

6. Leave the soap to set for 24 to 48 hours, or until the soap is solid and firm to the touch. Release the soap from the mold and allow to cure for 8 to 10 weeks.

14 ounces tepid water

5.5 ounces lye

40 ounces olive oil

the hand-milling method

To hand-mill simply means to grate, melt, and remold a basic cold-process soap to create a harder longer-lasting bar.

This is the part of the soap-making process where you can truly let your imagination fly. Now that the chemical reaction involving lye has taken place, you can freely add all sorts of ingredients to your soaps—cosmetic clay, cornmeal, citrus juice, glycerin, spices, cocoa butter, essential oils, herbal infusions and teas, wheat germ, vitamin E, aloe, goat's milk, honey, etc.—without worrying about how they might be affected by the lye. Expensive essential oils won't be wasted and will stay true to their original form and strength. Any added oils will only serve to enhance the soap—colors won't fade and fresh herbs won't lose any of their medicinal properties.

The hand-milling recipes in this book all call for forty ounces grated soap (one Basic Recipe batch) to twenty ounces liquid—water, herbal infusions, goat's milk, and so on. For the best results, hand-milled recipes require a top-quality Basic Recipe soap, but there is no reason why you shouldn't use the method to revitalize batches that haven't turned out quite as you'd planned—almost any batch can be improved by hand-milling; and you won't have to worry about curdling, seizure, refusal to trace, or separation.

Cold-process soap is ready to hand-mill anytime after two weeks of curing. (If you're not planning to mill cold-process batches, you must wait until the specified curing period is finished before you use the soap.) You can hand-mill soap whatever its age. Although you'll get the best results if you mill the soap while it is still young, that doesn't mean you won't get good results if you decide to mill a soap that's a year or more old. Remember to wear gloves when you are grating and handling the soap.

Be sure to gather your equipment, prepare all your ingredients, and set out your molds before you begin.

extra equipment—

hand-milling requires two extra pieces of equipment. As always with soap-making, once you've used this equipment for making soap, reserve it solely for this use, and do not use it in the preparation of food.

For grating the soap you will need a cheese grater—be sure it is good-quality: nice and sturdy. A food processor can be used if you want to speed up the process. A double boiler is also needed for melting the soap. You can improvise by fitting a stainless-steel mixing bowl inside a larger stock pot or saucepan. In fact, you may find that you can adapt your existing mixing pot for this purpose.

the method

1 Prepare your ingredients, and set out the molds.

2 In the top of a double boiler, heat the liquid ingredients to 180°F and add the grated soap.

3 Reduce the heat to a simmer, and melt the soap with a minimum of stirring, blending it into the liquid. Stirring and over-agitation of the melting mass will cause undesired foaming.

The objective is to attain a clear, watery appearance. If instead the mixture starts to thicken—so that it becomes too thick to pour—simply stir in the remaining ingredients and spoon the soap into the molds.

4 As soon as the mixture appears clear and watery, add the remaining ingredients and stir gently to blend.

5 Transfer the soap to a pouring pitcher and pour into the prepared molds.

6 Leave the soaps to cool to room temperature, until they have formed a thick skin or have become firm to the touch. Put the soaps into the freezer for 2 hours before popping them out of their molds. Allow them to dry in a warm well-ventilated area for 2 to 4 weeks.

the melt-&-pour method

Melt-and-pour soaps are quick and simple to make and are an ideal project for children. They are made of glycerin soap-base which, as the method-name suggests, is melted down and then poured into molds to harden. Once the glycerin is melted, you can easily add essential oils, botanicals, and dye (available as chips of color from any good craft store) to scent, color, and add interest to the soaps.

Glycerin soap-base comes in one-pound bags or blocks, and each pound will yield approximately six 2.5-ounce bars. To scent and color the soap-base, use half an ounce essential oil and one color chip per one pound glycerin.

the method

1 Prepare the mold or molds. As with cold-process soaps, you can pour the melted glycerin into a single mold, and slice the block into bars once it's set, or pour it into individual molds.

2 Set up a double boiler and bring the water to a simmer. Place the glycerin in the top and let it melt, skimming off any skin which forms on the surface of the melted glycerin.

3 Add the dye, essential oils or essential oil blend, and any other ingredients, and stir thoroughly.

4 Transfer the soap to a pouring pitcher, pour the soap into the prepared mold or molds, and leave to set for 30 minutes. Place the soap in the freezer for another 30 minutes, then remove and let the soap stand for 10 minutes more. Pop the soap out of the mold or molds. The soap is ready to use.

variations—one of the

wonderful things about melt-and-pour soaps is their translucency. Because glycerin is clear, you can simply and easily create all sorts of stunning visual effects. Anything you add—rose petals, rolled oats, lavender flowers, and so on—will all be clearly visible. There are some ideas in Chapter Four, but see what you can come up with! Melt-and-pour soaps are also much more versatile when it comes to the molds you can use, because you don't have to worry about lye-resistancy—so go out and see what creative molds you can find.

chapter two face

& body soaps

It's a wonderful thing—washing your face for the first time with a soap you've made yourself. You know exactly what's in it: no hidden chemicals and no hidden dyes—just good wholesome ingredients, carefully selected and lovingly blended.

This chapter is devoted to soaps for cleansing the face and body. You will find soaps that are suitable for the whole family—for both washing the body and shampooing the hair. (Just rub the soap over your hair, then work it up into a lather as you would regular shampoo, and rinse.) Then there are soaps for more specific needs: complexion soaps, moisturizing soaps, toning soaps, exfoliating soaps, soaps for problem skin, soaps for dry skin, and soaps that make you feel like you're bathing in lotion. Finally, there are soaps for shaving and soaps that are gentle enough for a baby's skin—whatever their age!

There is something here for everyone. And not only will these soaps fulfill their promise—to moisturize, cleanse, and soften—they will also smell delicious and fill your soul with feelings of well-being and contentment.

lavender & rosemary
shampoo & body bar

Lavender and rosemary are a classic pairing—as the lavender soothes and refreshes, the rosemary gently stimulates. And in this adaptation of Basic Recipe Two, they come together to make a richly lathered soap for the whole family. Use the bar to wash both your hair and body—while the herbs and aloe cleanse and condition, the castor and jojoba oils moisturize and soften.

1. Prepare the mold or molds.

2. Blend the water and lye. Set aside and cool to 100°F.

3. Melt the coconut and palm oils. Blend in the castor, olive, jojoba, and aloe vera oils and either heat or cool to 100°F.

4. Once the temperatures match, blend the lye solution into the oils.

5. Stir the mixture until the soap traces, then add the rosemary and lavender essential oils. Stir thoroughly and pour into the prepared mold or molds.

6. Leave the soap to set for 12 to 24 hours, or until the soap is solid and firm to the touch. Release the soap from the mold or molds and allow to cure for 4 to 6 weeks.

15 ounces tepid water

5.6 ounces lye

12 ounces coconut oil

6 ounces palm oil

10 ounces castor oil

8 ounces olive oil

3 ounces jojoba oil

1 ounce aloe vera oil

1 ounce rosemary essential oil

0.5 ounce lavender essential oil

An herb rich in folklore and tradition—rosemary has been prized for its medicinal properties for centuries. Rosemary essential oil is famed for its ability to stimulate the circulation and soothe away headaches and fatigue. In shampoos and hair rinses (see Chapter Four), rosemary deep-cleans hair follicles and treats hair and scalp problems, particularly dandruff.

patchouli complexion soap

Adapted from Basic Recipe Three, this recipe calls for a little less coconut oil, which creates a milder and less drying soap. The addition of astringent patchouli and healing aloe vera makes this a very good complexion soap for oily and problem skins that need a little soothing and extra help.

1. Prepare the mold or molds.

2. Blend the water and lye. Set aside and cool to 120°F.

3. Melt the coconut and palm oils. Blend in the olive oil and either heat or cool to 120°F.

4. Once the temperatures match, blend the lye solution into the oils.

5. Stir the mixture until the soap traces. Mix together the aloe vera oil and the patchouli essential oil, and add to the soap. Stir thoroughly and pour into the prepared mold or molds.

6. Leave the soap to set for 12 to 24 hours, or until the soap is solid and firm to the touch. Release the soap from the mold or molds and allow to cure for 6 to 8 weeks.

15 ounces tepid water

6.1 ounces lye

18 ounces coconut oil

4 ounces palm oil

16 ounces olive oil

2 ounces aloe vera oil

2 ounces patchouli essential oil

patchouli

Since the East first traded with the West, patchouli has been regarded with high esteem by both herbalists and perfumers. The essential oil is distilled from the leaves of the plant, which grows in Indonesia, China, and Madagascar. Patchouli has a woody, earthy smell that is sweet and spicy. The essential oil often appears as a bass note in commercial perfumes and has historically been used for the relief of problem skin.

calendula & cornmeal exfoliating bar

This is a wonderful exfoliating facial soap for sensitive skin. While the oatmeal works to unclog pores and gently scrubs away dead skin cells, the calendula soothes and softens. Adding the essential oil blend of lavender, clary sage, and cypress gives the soap a deliciously pungent fragrance—if calendula had a scent, this would be it.

1. Prepare the molds.

2. In the top of a double boiler, heat the water to 180°F and add the grated soap.

3. With a minimum of stirring, melt the soap.

4. When the soap and water have blended and the mixture is clear and runny, stir in the calendula-infused oil, the lavender, clary sage and cypress essential oils, the cornmeal, calendula petals, and turmeric. Pour into the prepared molds.

5. Leave the soaps to cool to room temperature, or until they have formed a thick skin and are firm to the touch. Release the soaps from their molds and allow to dry for 2 to 4 weeks.

18 ounces water

40 ounces Basic Recipe Four, grated

2 ounces calendula-infused oil (see page 99)

1 ounce lavender essential oil

0.5 ounce clary sage essential oil

0.5 ounce cypress essential oil

1 cup cornmeal

1 ounce dried calendula petals

0.5 teaspoon turmeric

sandalwood body bar

Suitable for normal to dry skin, this soap has a moisturizing lather which is imbued with the sensual aroma of sandalwood. Sandalwood essential oil is an emollient and mild astringent, and whether or not its fragrance is the aphrodisiac many believe it to be, it is certainly calming and relaxing.

1. Prepare the mold or molds.

2. Combine the sandalwood essential oil and the sandalwood powder; set aside.

3. Blend the water and lye. Set aside and cool to 95°F.

4. Melt the coconut and palm oils. Blend in the olive and wheat germ oils and either heat or cool to 95°F.

5. Once the temperatures match, blend the lye solution into the oils.

6. Stir the mixture until the soap traces, then add the sandalwood mixture. Stir thoroughly and pour into the prepared mold or molds.

7. Leave the soap to set for 18 to 24 hours, or until the soap is solid and firm to the touch. Release the soap from the mold or molds and allow to cure for 2 to 4 weeks.

2 ounces sandalwood essential oil

0.5 ounce sandalwood powder

14 ounces tepid water

6 ounces lye

18 ounces coconut oil

6 ounces palm oil

12 ounces olive oil

4 ounces wheat germ oil

sandalwood

For centuries, sandalwood has been one of the world's most treasured fragrances. Highly valued for its calming and relaxing qualities, and its exotic and luxurious scent, the oil is used in soaps, creams, and salves for helping to heal problem skin, and fungal and bacterial infections.

comfrey & lavender shaving soap

Shaving soaps are quickly becoming more and more popular, as the old mug-and-brush routine finds its way back into the American lifestyle. This mildly astringent and moisturizing shaving soap, with its old-fashioned fragrance of lavender, is a favorite that reminds many people of the soap their grandfather used to use.

1. Prepare the mold or molds.

2. Blend the water and lye. Set aside and cool to 100°F.

3. Melt the coconut and palm oils. Blend in the olive, castor, comfrey-infused, wheat germ, and aloe vera oils and either heat or cool to 100°F.

4. Once the temperatures match, blend the lye solution into the oils.

5. Stir the mixture until the soap traces, then add the lavender essential oil. Stir thoroughly and pour into the prepared mold or molds.

6. Leave the soap to set for 12 to 24 hours, or until the soap is solid and firm to the touch. Release the soap from the mold or molds and allow to cure for 2 to 4 weeks.

15 ounces tepid water

5.4 ounces lye

14 ounces coconut oil

6 ounces palm oil

6 ounces olive oil

4 ounces castor oil

4 ounces comfrey-infused oil (see page 99)

4 ounces wheat germ oil

2 ounces aloe vera oil

2 ounces lavender essential oil

Comfrey is also known as "boneknit" because the herb has traditionally been used in poultices for fractures. It has now been proven that comfrey speeds healing by encouraging cell growth. Soothing, emollient, and mildly astringent in nature, comfrey-infused oils and creams are useful for easing arthritic joints, muscle aches, and sprains.

glycerin & rosewater complexion soap

While glycerin moisturizes and protects the skin, rosewater provides gentle astringency—combining to create a complexion soap that is excellent for dry, sensitive skin. Use only fresh petals for this recipe, either rose or calendula—or both together. Make this soap when the roses are blooming, and add different colored petals to create a truly unique soap.

1. Prepare the molds.

2. In the top of a double boiler, heat the rosewater and glycerin to 180°F and add the grated soap.

3. With a minimum of stirring, melt the soap.

4. When the soap and liquids have blended and the mixture is clear and runny, stir in the petals, and the rose geranium essential oil. Pour into the prepared molds.

5. Leave the soaps to cool to room temperature, or until they have formed a thick skin and are firm to the touch. Release the soaps from their molds and allow to dry for 4 to 6 weeks.

16 ounces rosewater

4 ounces liquid glycerin

40 ounces Basic Recipe Two, grated

1 cup fresh rose and/or calendula petals

1 ounce rose geranium essential oil

The Glycerin and Rosewater Complexion Soaps, pictured here, were molded in silicon rubber molds, which are very durable and therefore worth the investment. Kits for making these molds are available from all good craft stores, and via mail order (see page 108).

goat's milk soap with avocado & dill

This is a creamy, emollient soap, enriched with soothing avocado oil and scented with the delicate fragrance of dill. Mild, gentle, and with a rich lather, this soap is excellent for cleansing very dry skin. Avocado oil is produced from the fruit's kernel and is included for its nourishing and conditioning qualities.

1. Prepare the molds.

2. In the top of a double boiler, heat the goat's milk, water, and avocado oil to 180°F and add the grated soap.

3. With a minimum of stirring, melt the soap.

4. When the soap and liquids have blended and the mixture is clear and runny, stir in the dillweed and essential oil. Pour into the prepared molds.

5. Leave the soaps to cool to room temperature, or until they have formed a thick skin and are firm to the touch. Release the soaps from their molds and allow to dry for 2 to 4 weeks.

10 ounces goat's milk

6 ounces water

4 ounces avocado oil

40 ounces Basic Recipe Five, grated

2 tablespoons finely chopped dried dillweed

0.5 ounce dill essential oil

chamomile & cornmeal soap

This soap combines the delightful and subtle fragrance of chamomile with the gentle scrubbing action of cornmeal. As the cornmeal cleanses and exfoliates, the profoundly calming quality of chamomile works its way through the lather, into your pores, and straight to the very core of your being—leaving you soothed and relaxed.

1. Prepare the molds.

2. Steep the chamomile tea bags in the boiling water for 5 minutes.

3. In the top of a double boiler, heat the chamomile tea and infused oil to 180°F and add the grated soap.

4. With a minimum of stirring, melt the soap.

5. When the soap and liquids have blended and the mixture is clear and runny, stir in the cornmeal and chamomile flowers. Pour into the prepared molds.

6. Leave the soaps to cool to room temperature, or until they have formed a thick skin and are firm to the touch. Release the soaps from their molds and allow to dry for 2 to 4 weeks.

4 chamomile tea bags

16 ounces boiling water

4 ounces chamomile-infused oil (see page 99)

40 ounces Basic Recipe Two, grated

1 cup yellow cornmeal (stone ground, if available)

1 ounce dried chamomile flowers, very finely chopped

Chamomile's mild astringency makes it very good for deep-cleaning pores: pour boiling water over some fresh leaves and flowers, and enjoy a facial sauna. The herb is also healing and wonderfully fragrant—drinking chamomile tea promotes relaxation and relief from indigestion. Once the tea's cooled down, use it as an eyewash for tired eyes and conjunctivitis. Chamomile-infused oils are excellent for treating eczema and insect bites.

lavender & oatmeal
exfoliating body bar

Chopped oats and whole lavender petals give this soap a truly unique look. Here, the oats gently exfoliate while the lavender adds a little extra spark that reaffirms that you are bathing with something very special. The sweet floral aroma soothes and balances—treat yourself to some lavender relaxation therapy.

1. Prepare the molds.

2. In the top of a double boiler, heat the water to 180°F and add the grated soap.

3. With a minimum of stirring, melt the soap.

4. When the soap and water have blended and the mixture is clear and runny, stir in the oats, and the lavender essential oil and flowers. Pour into the prepared molds.

5. Leave the soaps to cool to room temperature, or until they have formed a thick skin and are firm to the touch. Release the soaps from their molds and allow to dry for 2 to 4 weeks.

20 ounces water

40 ounces Basic Recipe One, grated

1 cup lightly chopped oats

2 ounces lavender essential oil

0.5 ounce whole lavender flowers

Lavender, with its purple-blue flowers and glorious scent, is one of the most widely available and popular herbs. The essential oil is distilled from the flowering tops of the plant and is extremely versatile. Among its many uses are the treatment of burns (a few drops mixed into a couple of ounces of aloe vera gel does wonderful things for relieving sunburn), cuts, bites, problem skin, headaches, insomnia, and asthma.

aloe & eucalyptus shampoo & body bar

Shampooing and bathing with this wonderful family soap will soon become a tradition. The fabled healing properties of aloe vera restore the skin's natural pH levels, while the eucalyptus stimulates and refreshes, creating a mild tingling sensation as the circulation to the skin and hair follicles is invigorated.

1. Prepare the mold or molds.

2. Mix together the aloe vera leaf and aloe vera gel; set aside.

3. Blend the water and lye. Set aside and cool to 100°F.

4. Melt the coconut and palm oils. Blend in the castor, olive, jojoba, wheat germ, and aloe vera oils and either heat or cool to 100°F.

5. Once the temperatures match, blend the lye solution into the oils.

6. Stir the mixture until the soap traces, then add the aloe vera mixture and the eucalyptus essential oil. Stir thoroughly and pour into the prepared mold or molds.

7. Leave the soap to set for 12 to 24 hours, or until the soap is solid and firm to the touch. Release the soap from the mold or molds and allow to cure for 6 to 8 weeks.

3 tablespoons liquefied fresh aloe vera leaf

1 tablespoon aloe vera gel

14 ounces tepid water

5.6 ounces lye

10 ounces coconut oil

6 ounces palm oil

10 ounces castor oil

6 ounces olive oil

3 ounces jojoba oil

3 ounces wheat germ oil

2 ounces aloe vera oil

2 ounces eucalyptus essential oil

Magical aloe vera has been renowned for its healing powers since ancient times. The plant is very easy to grow, providing a ready supply of fresh leaves and gel. Apply the gel directly to cuts and burns for instant pain relief. Because the plant is mostly water, and does not contain much oil, aloe vera oil is actually a blend of aloe oil and another vegetable oil, usually soy. Aloe vera oil is available from the specialty oil suppliers listed on page 108.

vitamin e shaving soap scented with bay & rum

Bay, rum, orange, cinnamon, and allspice—the bold flavors and heady scents of the Caribbean come together in this shaving soap which has a surprisingly delicate fragrance. Vitamin E is added for its soothing, emollient nature.

1. Mix together the rum, allspice, cinnamon, and the bay and sweet orange essential oils, and seal in a jar. Set aside for 48 hours, so that the fragrances can blend together and mellow.

2. Prepare the molds.

3. Strain the rum mixture through a fine-mesh strainer, reserving the rum.

4. In the top of a double boiler, heat the water and rum to 180°F and add the grated soap.

5. With a minimum of stirring, melt the soap.

6. When the soap and liquids have blended and the mixture is clear and runny, stir in the vitamin E. Pour into the prepared molds.

7. Leave the soaps to cool to room temperature, or until they have formed a thick skin and are firm to the touch. Release the soaps from their molds and allow to dry for 4 to 6 weeks.

2 ounces dark Jamaican rum

1 heaping tablespoon ground allspice

1 heaping tablespoon ground cinnamon

1 ounce bay essential oil

1 ounce sweet orange essential oil

18 ounces water

40 ounces Basic Recipe One, grated

2 ounces vitamin E

Frequently used in cosmetics and skin lotions, vitamin E is beneficial in healing cuts and abrasions, and is also believed to have anti-aging properties. When you buy the vitamin E for this recipe, ask for 1,000 I. U. per gram, d-alpha tocopheryl—which may sound complicated, but it just means that you get pure vitamin E (all the other varieties are synthetically produced). It's available in good health food stores.

tangerine moisturizer bar

This extremely gentle exfoliating soap for dry skin is kind enough to use on your face. Loaded with moisturizing oils and a wonderful citrusy fragrance, this soap will leave your skin feeling refreshed and invigorated. The tangerine essential oil is lightly astringent and delicately removes dead skin cells, while the soap's creamy lather allows the oils to penetrate and moisturize your skin.

1. Prepare the mold or molds.

2. Blend the water and lye. Set aside and cool to 100°F.

3. Melt the coconut and palm oils, and the cocoa butter. Blend in the olive, castor, jojoba, and wheat germ oils and either heat or cool to 100°F.

4. Once the temperatures match, blend the lye solution into the oils.

5. Stir the mixture until the soap traces, then add the tangerine essential oil, and the turmeric and paprika. Stir thoroughly and pour into the prepared mold or molds.

6. Leave the soap to set for 12 to 24 hours, or until the soap is solid and firm to the touch. Release the soap from the mold or molds and allow to cure for 4 to 6 weeks.

14 ounces tepid water

5.4 ounces lye

12 ounces coconut oil

4 ounces palm oil

2 ounces cocoa butter

8 ounces olive oil

6 ounces castor oil

4 ounces jojoba oil

4 ounces wheat germ oil

2 ounces tangerine essential oil

1 tablespoon turmeric

1 teaspoon paprika

sandalwood & rosin soap

The rare and exotic fragrance of sandalwood, and the cleansing qualities of rosin, combine to create a sensuous soap with a generous lather that gently scrubs the skin while deep-cleaning the pores. Calming and cooling, this soap will leave you feeling pampered and relaxed.

1. Prepare the molds.

2. In the top of a double boiler, heat the water to 180°F and add the grated soap.

3. With a minimum of stirring, melt the soap.

4. When the soap and water have blended and the mixture is clear and runny, stir in the rosin, and the sandalwood essential oil and powder. Pour into the prepared molds.

5. Leave the soaps to cool to room temperature, or until they have formed a thick skin and are firm to the touch. Release the soaps from their molds and allow to dry for 2 to 4 weeks.

20 ounces water

40 ounces Basic Recipe One, grated

2 ounces rosin

2 ounces sandalwood essential oil

2 ounces sandalwood powder

Rosin is the fine, powdery residue that is the by-product of the distillation of pine resins. Useful in soap-making because it helps dried bars of soap retain their shape (so you can get to work and find some really ambitious molds for this soap!) rosin also produces large amounts of lather; so bathing with a soap that includes rosin is a truly luxurious experience.

green herbs baby soap

Plantain and chickweed may be two of the most prolific garden weeds, but they are also two herbs that have long histories of soothing and healing—they are actually far more valuable than the lawns they blemish! Here they work together to create a very mild soap with a creamy lather—washing with this soap feels like you are bathing in lotion.

1. Prepare the molds.

2. In the top of a double boiler, heat the water and infused oil to 180°F and add the grated soap.

3. With a minimum of stirring, melt the soap.

4. When the soap and liquids have blended and the mixture is clear and runny, pour into the prepared molds.

5. Leave the soaps to cool to room temperature, or until they have formed a thick skin and are firm to the touch. Release the soaps from their molds and allow to dry for 2 to 4 weeks.

17 ounces water

3 ounces chickweed-and-plantain-infused oil (see page 99)

40 ounces Basic Recipe Two, grated

Astringent plantain and soothing chickweed—which help to cure skin inflammations, including chafing and diaper rash—combine in this glorious soap. The wonderful green color is the result of the chlorophyll infused into the plantain and chickweed oil.

moisturizing goat's milk & ylang-ylang bar

For centuries, goat's milk has been valued for its cleansing and moisturizing properties—teaming it with jojoba and cocoa butter creates a soap with an exceptionally creamy lather. Ylang-ylang is included for its ability to stimulate and tone the skin, as well as to give the soap its wonderful fragrance—which is very relaxing and reputed to be an aphrodisiac.

1. Prepare the mold or molds.

2. Melt the coconut and palm oils, and the cocoa butter. Blend in the olive and jojoba oils and either heat or cool to 110°F.

3. Blend the goat's milk and lye, stirring to dissolve the lye.

4. Before the lye solution turns orange, blend it into the oils.

5. Stir the mixture until the soap traces, then add the ylang-ylang essential oil. Stir thoroughly and pour into the prepared mold or molds.

6. Leave the soap to set for 18 to 24 hours, or until the soap is solid and firm to the touch. Release the soap from the mold or molds and allow to cure for 4 to 6 weeks.

22 ounces coconut oil

6 ounces palm oil

2 ounces cocoa butter

6 ounces olive oil

4 ounces jojoba oil

14 ounces goat's milk

6 ounces lye

2 ounces ylang-ylang essential oil

rosemary & geranium
complexion soap

This is a mild, beautifully scented, yellow-green soap with excellent lather. Suitable for combination skin, the rosemary and geranium essential oils are versatile astringents—powerful enough to cleanse and dry the oily zones, while soothing and moisturizing the drier areas.

1. Prepare the molds.

2. In the top of a double boiler, heat the water to 180°F and add the grated soap.

3. With a minimum of stirring, melt the soap.

4. When the soap and water have blended and the mixture is clear and runny, stir in the ground rosemary, and the geranium and rosemary essential oils. Pour into the prepared molds.

5. Leave the soaps to cool to room temperature, or until they have formed a thick skin and are firm to the touch. Release the soaps from their molds and allow to dry for 2 to 4 weeks.

20 ounces water

40 ounces Basic Recipe Two, grated

2 tablespoons ground rosemary

1 ounce geranium essential oil

1 ounce rosemary essential oil

Widely used in skin care products by the cosmetics industry, geranium essential oil is valued for its cleansing astringency and antiseptic properties; as well as for its delicious, leafy aroma. Distilled from the rose geranium plant, this essential oil also has the ability to calm and soothe inflammations. A few drops added to a warm bath does wonders for easing the pain of cystitis.

calendula & sage baby soap

This is called a baby soap because it is gentle enough to use on a baby's sensitive skin—but that means sensitive skin of any age! This soap is truly mild and combines the soothing qualities of calendula with the healing powers of sage in a creamy lather that is wonderful for skin that needs a little extra care.

1. Prepare the mold or molds.

2. Blend the water and lye. Set aside and cool to 100°F.

3. Melt the coconut oil. Blend in the calendula-infused, castor and wheat germ oils and either heat or cool to 100°F.

4. Once the temperatures match, blend the lye solution into the oils.

5. Stir the mixture until the soap traces, then add the calendula petals and sage essential oil. Stir thoroughly and pour into the prepared mold or molds.

6. Leave the soap to set for 24 to 36 hours, or until the soap is solid and firm to the touch. Release the soap from the mold or molds and allow to cure for 4 to 6 weeks.

15 ounces tepid water

5.9 ounces lye

16 ounces coconut oil

16 ounces calendula-infused oil (see page 99)

4 ounces castor oil

4 ounces wheat germ oil

1 ounce fresh or dried calendula petals

1 ounce sage essential oil

calendula

The brightly-colored flowers of this herb, which is often called by its other name, Pot Marigold, produce an astringent and strongly antiseptic infused oil that is excellent for healing cuts, calluses, and skin inflammations, especially eczema and diaper rash. (Calendula has long been used by the pharmaceutical industry in creams and salves for diaper rash.) Adding twenty to thirty drops of the oil to a bath will help soothe away tension, anxiety, and depression.

chapter three

working soaps

From the moment it was discovered that lye solution mixed with oil saponified into soap, soap-makers have created recipes for specific needs. Soap-making satisfaction is multiplied as soon as you begin using a soap that you've crafted for a purpose other than smelling good and lathering well.

This chapter is full of recipes for soaps that will go to work for you in your home. There are soaps for scrubbing your pots and pans, and washing your laundry, general household soaps, and soaps with even more specific purposes.

Use one of the kitchen soaps, for example, to keep cooking hands odor-free and sanitary; or try one of the soaps designed to wash away earth and grit from the garden and then to heal any nicks and cuts collected along the way. There is even a soap to soothe the pain and irritation of poison ivy; and another that will temporarily remove human scent and allow you to stroll through the wilderness without disturbing wildlife. Others will deter insects from biting and stinging you and your pets. Lastly, there are soaps for when your hands get truly dirty—be they greasy, grimy, or oil-stained, there is a recipe here that can help you clean up after every messy chore.

laundry soaps

recipe one

This is a simple and effective liquid soap that you use the same way as a liquid detergent. If you like, you can add essential oils to this recipe—just remember that all of your laundry will smell of their fragrance! Here, patchouli is added because it is an effective moth-deterrent. Use patchouli laundry soap when it's time to wash your summer or winter clothes, before packing them away for the season.

1. Prepare the containers—you will need four 10-ounce bottles.

2. In the top of a double boiler, combine the water and grated soap. Gently heat until the soap has melted and the liquid is clear and runny.

3. Add the patchouli essential oil, blend well, and pour into the prepared containers.

40 ounces water

10 ounces Basic Recipe One or Six, grated

20 drops patchouli or other essential oil, if desired

recipe two

Alternatively, put grated soap directly into your washing machine. Handmade soaps take a little longer to dissolve than powder detergents, so dissolve the soap in a little water first. If you are doing a white wash, you can also add some bluing or borax. This recipe makes enough for one washing-machine load.

1. In a bowl, mix together the soap, water, and bluing or borax if using. Set aside for a few minutes.

2. Pour the soap mixture on top of your laundry in the washing machine.

3. Run the washing machine on its usual cycle.

1 cup grated Basic Recipe One or Six

16 ounces water

2 tablespoons bluing or borax, if using

dish washing soap

Now is your chance to melt down any less-than-successful batches of soap into this effective dish washing liquid. Alternatively, Basic Recipe One will do just fine. The sweet orange and rosemary essential oils are included for their grease-cutting power; but you could use any other essential oil—lavender, sage, or patchouli: they would all make excellent additions. Add them one drop at a time until you achieve the desired scent.

1. Prepare the containers—you will need four 10-ounce bottles.

2. Combine the water and grated soap in the top of a double boiler. Gently heat until the soap has melted and the liquid is clear and runny.

3. Add the glycerin, and the rosemary and sweet orange essential oils. Blend well and pour the soap into the prepared containers.

40 ounces water

16 ounces Basic Recipe One, grated

4 ounces liquid glycerin

1 ounce rosemary essential oil

1 ounce sweet orange essential oil

southern citrus kitchen soap

The odor-cutting abilities of citrus essential oils makes this a particularly useful hand soap to keep beside your kitchen sink. Odors and bacteria from garlic, onion, seafood, and meat will all be washed away, leaving only the delicate, refreshing scent of citrus. To replace the moisture that cooking steam and citrus acids leach out, moisturizing oils are also added.

1. Prepare the mold or molds.

2. Blend the water and lye. Set aside and cool to 100°F.

3. Melt the coconut oil. Blend in the olive, aloe vera, castor, jojoba, and wheat germ oils and either heat or cool to 100°F.

4. Once the temperatures match, blend the lye solution into the oils.

5. Stir the mixture until the soap traces, then add the sweet orange, lemon, grapefruit, and lime essential oils, and the lime zest. Stir thoroughly and pour into the prepared mold or molds.

6. Leave the soap to set for 18 to 24 hours, or until the soap is solid and firm to the touch. Release the soap from the mold or molds and allow to cure for 2 to 4 weeks.

15 ounces tepid water

5.8 ounces lye

16 ounces coconut oil

10 ounces olive oil

2 ounces aloe vera oil

2 ounces castor oil

2 ounces jojoba oil

2 ounces wheat germ oil

2 ounces sweet orange essential oil

1 ounce lemon essential oil

0.5 ounce grapefruit essential oil

0.5 ounce lime essential oil

1 ounce powdered or fine granular dried lime zest

tarragon & geranium
household soap

This is a useful soap to keep around the house—make lots of small bars and place one beside every hand-washing sink. The soap has a delicate light pink color flecked with green pieces of tarragon, and its delicious floral aroma is always popular. Geranium essential oil ensures that the soap will cleanse without drying.

1. Prepare the mold or molds.

2. Blend the water and lye. Set aside and cool to 100°F.

3. Melt the coconut and palm oils. Blend in the olive oil and either heat or cool to 100°F.

4. Once the temperatures match, blend the lye solution into the oils.

5. Stir the mixture until the soap traces, then add the geranium, rosewood, and tarragon essential oils, the tarragon leaves, and the paprika and turmeric. Stir thoroughly and pour into the prepared mold or molds.

6. Leave the soap to set for 12 to 18 hours, or until the soap is solid and firm to the touch. Release the soap from the mold or molds and allow to cure for 2 to 4 weeks.

14 ounces tepid water

5.9 ounces lye

18 ounces coconut oil

6 ounces palm oil

16 ounces olive oil

1 ounce geranium essential oil

0.5 ounce rosewood essential oil

0.5 ounce tarragon essential oil

2 tablespoons finely chopped dried tarragon leaves

2 teaspoons paprika

1 teaspoon turmeric

spiced oat bar

On those occasions when a little extra scrubbing is needed to clean away the residue—even the worst grease, grime, and oil—of a particularly grubby task, this is the soap to use. Chopped oats provide the cleaning power, while the spices give the soap a beautifully rich, dark brown color. Chop the oats in a food processor or spice grinder to a medium-chunky powder.

1. Prepare the molds.

2. In the top of a double boiler, heat the water to 180°F, and add the grated soap.

3. With a minimum of stirring, melt the soap.

4. When the soap and water has blended and the mixture is clear and runny, stir in the oats, the cinnamon, allspice, and nutmeg, and the rosemary, sage, and clove essential oils. Pour into the prepared molds.

5. Leave the soaps to cool to room temperature, or until they have formed a thick skin and are firm to the touch. Release the soaps from their molds and allow to dry for 2 to 4 weeks.

20 ounces water

40 ounces Basic Recipe Two, grated

2 cups finely chopped oats

4 tablespoons ground cinnamon

2 tablespoons ground allspice

2 tablespoons ground nutmeg

0.5 ounce rosemary essential oil

0.5 ounce sage essential oil

0.25 ounce clove essential oil

Oats, oatmeal, and cornmeal—these are the most commonly used grains in soap-making. Their cleansing action is legendary, and because of their high silica content they are believed to be effective in helping to clear up many skin conditions, particularly eczema. They are all readily available in grocery stores, health food stores, and food co-ops—select organic varieties whenever possible.

basil & sun-dried tomato soap

The ingredients in this soap, besides having a strong culinary appeal, are exactly what make it so effective in the kitchen. Basil essential oil is very antibacterial and can destroy the common causes of food-borne illness, including salmonella. The basil leaves and little bits of sun-dried tomato provide gentle scrubbing, helping to keep cooking hands clean. Try to avoid the temptation of serving this one up for dinner!

1. Prepare the mold or molds.

2. Blend the water and lye. Set aside and cool to 100°F.

3. Melt the coconut and palm oils. Blend in the olive and jojoba oils and either heat or cool to 100°F.

4. Once the temperatures match, blend the lye solution into the oils.

5. Stir the mixture until the soap traces, then add the basil essential oil, the sun-dried tomatoes, and the basil leaves. Stir thoroughly and pour into the prepared mold or molds.

6. Leave the soap to set for 12 to 18 hours, or until the soap is solid and firm to the touch. Release the soap from the mold or molds and allow to cure for 2 to 4 weeks.

14 ounces tepid water

5.8 ounces lye

18 ounces coconut oil

6 ounces palm oil

12 ounces olive oil

4 ounces jojoba oil

1 ounce basil essential oil

1 ounce dry-packed sun-dried tomatoes, finely chopped

2 tablespoons finely chopped dried basil leaves

When searching for fresh botanicals to add to your soap recipes, the farmers' market is a good place to start—although seasonal, fresh herbs and flowers, fruits and vegetables are readily available.

licorice soap

This is always a favorite because its smell invariably evokes fond childhood memories of licorice candy. On a more practical note, the anise and sweet fennel essential oils in this recipe also have strong antibacterial properties, which make this a very useful household soap; particularly in the kitchen when you are preparing raw fish or meat.

1. Prepare the mold or molds.

2. Blend the water and lye. Set aside and cool to 100°F.

3. Melt the coconut and palm oils. Blend in the olive oil and either heat or cool to 100°F.

4. Once the temperatures match, blend the lye solution into the oils.

5. Stir the mixture until the soap traces, then add the anise and sweet fennel essential oils, the fennel seed and anise. Stir thoroughly and pour into the prepared mold or molds.

6. Leave the soap to set for 12 to 18 hours, or until the soap is solid and firm to the touch. Release the soap from the mold or molds and allow to cure for 2 to 4 weeks.

14.5 ounces tepid water

5.9 ounces lye

18 ounces coconut oil

6 ounces palm oil

16 ounces olive oil

1 ounce anise essential oil

0.5 ounce sweet fennel essential oil

1 tablespoon coarsely ground fennel seed

1 teaspoon ground anise seed or star anise

Strange as it may seem, licorice soap is popular with fishermen. They have discovered that not only does the smell of licorice mask human odor, but that fish are attracted to it! Several companies now produce licorice-scented sprays for coating fish lures.

deepwoods bar

The concentration of bug-repelling essential oils in this soap will deter mosquitoes and other biting and stinging insects. You can grate this soap and use it to launder clothes (see page 70), as well as wash and shampoo with it. Don't be put off by the strong smell of the freshly made soap. The aroma mellows as it cures, but do cure it separately from other soaps; you don't want them picking up any unwanted aromas!

1. Prepare the mold or molds.

2. Blend the water and lye. Set aside and cool to 100°F.

3. Melt the coconut and palm oils. Blend in the olive, aloe vera, jojoba, and castor oils and either heat or cool to 100°F.

4. Once the temperatures match, blend the lye solution into the oils.

5. Stir the mixture until the soap traces, then add the citronella, eucalyptus, lavender, peppermint, bergamot, and lemongrass essential oils. Stir thoroughly and pour into the prepared mold or molds.

6. Leave the soap to set for 18 to 24 hours, or until the soap is solid and firm to the touch. Release the soap from the mold or molds and allow to cure for 2 to 4 weeks.

14.5 ounces tepid water

5.8 ounces lye

18 ounces coconut oil

6 ounces palm oil

6 ounces olive oil

4 ounces aloe vera oil

4 ounces jojoba oil

2 ounces castor oil

2 ounces citronella essential oil

1 ounce eucalyptus essential oil

1 ounce lavender essential oil

1 ounce peppermint essential oil

0.5 ounce bergamot essential oil

0.5 ounce lemongrass essential oil

pet shampoo

This soap contains four essential oils that will repel fleas and ticks from your pet. Additionally, the healing properties of aloe and the moisturizing qualities of jojoba combine to ensure that your dog or cat has a healthy, shiny coat. This soap has a pungent aroma, so cure and store it separately from other soaps.

1. Prepare the mold or molds.

2. Blend the water and lye. Set aside and cool to 100°F.

3. Melt the coconut and palm oils. Blend in the olive, castor, jojoba, and aloe vera oils and either heat or cool to 100°F.

4. Once the temperatures match, blend the lye solution into the oils.

5. Stir the mixture until the soap traces, then add the cedar, citronella, eucalyptus, and pennyroyal essential oils. Stir thoroughly and pour into the prepared mold or molds.

6. Leave the soap to set for 18 to 24 hours, or until the soap is solid and firm to the touch. Release the soap from the mold or molds and allow to cure for 2 to 4 weeks.

15 ounces tepid water

6 ounces lye

16 ounces coconut oil

4 ounces palm oil

10 ounces olive oil

4 ounces castor oil

4 ounces jojoba oil

2 ounces aloe vera oil

0.5 ounce cedar essential oil

0.5 ounce citronella essential oil

0.5 ounce eucalyptus essential oil

0.5 ounce pennyroyal essential oil

Distilled from the leaves and twigs of the eucalyptus tree, eucalyptus essential oil is one of the most effective and popular oils. Antiseptic, antibacterial, and antiviral, it is often used in vaporizers, inhalants, and lozenges. Invaluable during cold and flu season, eucalyptus essential oil works to soothe sore throats and treat coughs—try simmering some eucalyptus leaves in a cast-iron pot on top of a wood-burning stove during those dark and dreary winter days.

camouflage bar

Bathe with this soap and you will be able to walk in the woods without alarming the animals—the essence of trees will allow you to blend invisibly into the breeze. Oakmoss absolute has the subtle fragrance of the forest, while the birch and white oak barks are strongly astringent and temporarily remove the oils that carry human scent—a quality that Native Americans discovered thousands of years ago.

1. Bring the water to a boil. In a bowl, pour it over the white oak and birch barks. Leave to cool to room temperature.

2. Prepare the mold or molds.

3. Dissolve the oakmoss absolute in the frazer fir and spruce essential oils.

4. Strain the bark tea and blend with the lye. Set aside and cool to 100°F.

5. Melt the coconut and palm oils. Blend in the olive oil and either heat or cool to 100°F.

6. Once the temperatures match, blend the lye solution into the oils.

7. Stir the mixture until the soap traces, then add the oakmoss absolute mixture. Stir thoroughly and pour into the prepared mold or molds.

8. Leave the soap to set for 18 to 24 hours, or until the soap is solid and firm to the touch. Release the soap from the mold or molds and allow to cure for 2 to 4 weeks.

16 ounces water

2 ounces white oak bark

2 ounces birch bark

0.5 ounce oakmoss absolute, warmed to room temperature

1 ounce frazer fir essential oil

1 ounce spruce essential oil

5.9 ounces lye

20 ounces coconut oil

6 ounces palm oil

14 ounces olive oil

Oakmoss absolute, which is widely used in the perfume industry, and white oak and birch barks provide the concealing magic in this soap. Anywhere that sells essential oils will be able to supply them. Oakmoss has a sticky consistency at room temperature and is difficult to work with. So, warm the oakmoss container in hot water before weighing.

gardener's grits bar

Lemongrass, geranium, and patchouli blend in this recipe to create a wonderfully special fragrance that will make even the most reluctant "green thumbs" want to get dirty—just so they can clean up afterwards with this soap. The abrasive action is provided by stone-ground corn grits.

1. Prepare the mold or molds.

2. Blend the water and lye. Set aside and cool to 100°F.

3. Melt the coconut and palm oils. Blend in the olive oil and either heat or cool to 100°F.

4. Once the temperatures match, blend the lye solution into the oils.

5. Stir the mixture until the soap traces, then add the grits and the geranium, patchouli, and lemongrass essential oils. Stir thoroughly and pour into the prepared mold or molds.

6. Leave the soap to set for 12 to 18 hours, or until the soap is solid and firm to the touch. Release the soap from the mold or molds and allow to cure for 2 to 4 weeks.

15.8 ounces tepid water

5.8 ounces lye

20 ounces coconut oil

6 ounces palm oil

14 ounces olive oil

4 ounces stone-ground corn grits

1 ounce geranium essential oil

1 ounce patchouli essential oil

0.5 ounce lemongrass
essential oil

sage & aloe garden bar

The addition of a little sand makes this soap lightly abrasive, so it is excellent for scrubbing away stubborn garden soil from the little cracks in your hands. Its rich, thick lather contains the moisture-replacing qualities of jojoba, and combines the astringent action of sage with the healing magic of aloe.

1. Prepare the mold or molds.

2. Blend the water and lye. Set aside and cool to 100°F.

3. Melt the coconut and palm oils. Blend in the olive, aloe vera, and jojoba oils and either heat or cool to 100°F.

4. Once the temperatures match, blend the lye solution into the oils.

5. Stir the mixture until the soap traces, then add the sage essential oil, the sand, aloe vera leaf, and the rubbed sage. Stir thoroughly and pour into the prepared mold or molds.

6. Leave the soap to set for 12 to 18 hours, or until the soap is solid and firm to the touch. Release the soap from the mold or molds and allow to cure for 4 to 6 weeks.

15 ounces tepid water

5.6 ounces lye

16 ounces coconut oil

4 ounces palm oil

12 ounces olive oil

6 ounces aloe vera oil

2 ounces jojoba oil

2 ounces sage essential oil

1 ounce clean play sand

2 tablespoons finely chopped fresh aloe vera leaf

2 tablespoons rubbed sage leaves

Sage is very astringent and antiseptic. It has been valued since ancient times for its medicinal properties, particularly for healing wounds. The essential oil is a powerful stimulant and often used to treat people who have been worn down by stress or overwork.

jewelweed soap

For centuries, jewelweed has been the traditional remedy for soothing the discomfort associated with poison oak and poison ivy; and the remedy works just as well in this soap. Use only the fresh leaves and tender upper stems when you extract the juice (using a juicer works best) and make the tea.

12 ounces fresh jewelweed

Water

8 ounces jewelweed juice

40 ounces Basic Recipe Two, grated

1. To prepare the jewelweed tea, place the jewelweed in a 2-quart saucepan and cover with water. Bring the water to a boil. Reduce the heat and simmer until the liquid is reduced by half, then strain. Measure out 12 ounces tea and discard the remainder.

2. Prepare your molds.

3. In the top of a double boiler, heat the jewelweed tea and juice to 180°F and add the grated soap.

4. With a minimum of stirring, melt the soap.

5. When the soap and water has blended, and the mixture is clear and runny, pour into the prepared molds.

6. Leave the soaps to cool to room temperature, or until they have formed a thick skin and are firm to the touch. Release the soaps from their molds and allow to dry for 4 to 6 weeks.

Jewelweed is native to North America where its ability to ease the pain of poison oak and poison ivy was discovered by Native Americans thousands of years ago. Prolific and fast-growing, jewelweed is also known as "touch-me-not."

chapter four

specialty soaps

On the following pages you will find recipes for soaps that are a little bit extra-special. These are recipes that will take your soap-making skills and knowledge one step further, and hopefully encourage you to experiment and try out your own ideas.

In this chapter, there are beautiful soaps that make luxurious and enticing gifts—if your friends haven't already been begging for bars of your delicious handmade soap, they will be now! These soaps will wake you up, calm you down, refresh, revive, cool, soothe, ease away aches and pains, restore or rejuvenate.

There are also recipes for bath oil, shower gel, bath bags, herbal rinses, and herb-infused oils—not soaps at all but recipes that fully utilize the attributes of oils, essential oils, and herbs.

Finally, there is the precursor to it all. Before there was ever a temple on Mount Sapo and the knowledge to make cold-process soap, there was soapwort. Used by the ancients for its natural cleansing power, soapwort is the original cleaning agent; and at the end of this chapter there are recipes that introduce you to this wonderful, bubbly ingredient.

glycerin soaps

Glycerin soaps always make attractive and welcome gifts—translucent, deliciously scented, beautifully colored, and wonderful to use. Enchanting as they already are, the following recipes are designed to give you other ideas, so you can create your own splendid variations on these themes. Use one-pound-capacity molds, and choose your own colors, essential oils, and botanicals.

layered soap

1. In the top of a double boiler, melt the glycerin soap-base.

2. Add the dye and essential oil. Stir well, then pour three-quarters of the soap into the prepared mold. Return the unpoured soap to the heat and allow the poured soap to set for 5 minutes.

3. Add the botanicals to the unpoured soap and stir well. Pour the remaining soap into the mold.

4. Leave the soap to set for 30 minutes, then place in the freezer for another 30 minutes. Let stand for 10 minutes, then pop the soap out of the mold.

1 pound glycerin soap-base

1 color chip

0.5 ounces essential oil

0.5 cup rolled oats or lavender flowers, or 1 cup rose petals

fragmented soap

1. In the top of a double boiler, melt the glycerin soap-base.

2. Add the first color chip and half the essential oil. Stir well, then pour into the prepared mold.

3. Once cooled and unmolded (as described above), cut the soap into small strips.

4. Follow steps 1 and 2 with the remaining ingredients.

5. Quickly stir in the soap pieces, leave to set, and unmold as above.

1 pound glycerin soap-base

0.5 color chip, first color

0.5 ounce essential oil

0.5 color chip, second color

chocolate-mint mousse soap

This sumptuous soap looks good enough to eat and makes a wonderful gift. The soap is poured into a single large mold in three phases, giving the finished bars a layered look—just like a fancy dessert! Melt the chocolate over medium heat in the top of a double boiler, and be sure to keep the melted chocolates warm, so they stay melted but do not continue cooking.

1. Prepare the mold.

2. Melt the white chocolate with 1 ounce of the olive oil. Blend in the cocoa powder, then set aside in a warm place.

3. Melt the dark chocolate with 1 ounce of the olive oil. Set aside in a warm place.

4. Blend the water and lye. Set aside and cool to 110°F.

5. Melt the coconut and palm oils, and the cocoa butter. Blend in the remaining 14 ounces olive oil and either heat or cool to 110°F.

6. Once the temperatures match, blend the lye solution into the oils.

7. Stir the mixture until the soap traces, then add the peppermint essential oil. Stir thoroughly, and pour enough soap into the prepared mold to fill one-third of the mold.

8. Add the white chocolate mixture to the soap and blend in lightly. (You may get a slightly marbled effect.) Pour half the soap into the mold.

9. Add the dark chocolate to the remaining soap and blend in thoroughly. Pour the soap into the mold.

10. Leave the soap to set for 24 to 36 hours, or until the soap is solid and firm to the touch. Release the soap from the mold and allow to cure for 4 to 6 weeks.

2 ounces white chocolate

16 ounces olive oil

0.25 cup cocoa powder

1 ounce dark chocolate

15 ounces tepid water

6 ounces lye

18 ounces coconut oil

4 ounces palm oil

2 ounces cocoa butter

1 ounce peppermint essential oil

espresso soap

This is another soap that is delightful for gift-giving—especially to those who love coffee. The soap has a beautiful rich-brown color, but beware—the delicious aroma of coffee may keep you awake for weeks as the soap cures! Use espresso or other very finely-ground, dark-roasted beans; they are roasted longer than other beans and will give the soap a darker color and a more robust, flavorful aroma.

1. Combine the coffee with the Everclear and Kahlua. Tightly seal the mixture in a small jar and leave to stand for 24 hours.

2. Prepare the mold or molds.

3. Blend the water and lye. Set aside and cool to 120°F.

4. Melt the coconut and palm oils. Blend in the olive oil and either heat or cool to 120°F.

5. Once the temperatures match, blend the lye solution into the oils.

6. Stir the mixture until the soap traces, then add the coffee mixture. Stir thoroughly and pour into the prepared mold or molds.

7. Leave the soap to set for 24 to 36 hours, or until the soap is solid and firm to the touch. Release the soap from the mold or molds and allow to cure for 4 to 6 weeks.

1 cup finely ground coffee beans

0.5 ounce Everclear or grain alcohol

0.5 ounce Kahlua or other coffee liqueur

14 ounces tepid water

6 ounces lye

14 ounces coconut oil

6 ounces palm oil

20 ounces olive oil

lavender ice

This recipe sounds trumpets for the noble herb lavender, which imparts a sensual aroma and blue-green color to this beautiful soap. Use Basic Recipe One—and for best results make this recipe within three to six days of preparing the basic soap, rather than waiting for the soap to cure for two weeks. Make sure you wear gloves when you handle the soap—it will still be highly alkaline.

1. In a food processor, combine the lavender and Everclear and process at high speed for 2 minutes. Pour into a jar, seal tightly, and let stand for at least 24 hours.

2. Prepare the molds.

3. Strain the lavender and alcohol mixture. Place the liquid and grated soap in the top of a double boiler.

4. With a minimum of stirring, melt the soap.

5. When the soap and liquid have blended and the mixture is clear and runny, stir in the lavender essential oil. Pour into the prepared molds.

6. Leave the soaps to cool to room temperature, or until they have formed a thick skin and are firm to the touch. Release the soaps from their molds and allow to dry for 4 to 6 weeks.

1 cup finely minced fresh lavender

20 ounces Everclear or grain alcohol

40 ounces Basic Recipe One, grated

1 ounce lavender essential oil

You can use this recipe as the basis for creating all sorts of beautiful soaps. Just substitute other herbs, such as rosemary or sage, for the lavender and prepare the alcohol extraction in the same way. You can also use fresh produce: strawberries, peaches, and cucumbers, for example, and follow exactly the same method as that above.

peppermint & tea tree wake-up bar

This soap is your wake-up call on those mornings when the last thing you want to do is get out of bed. While the tea tree oil will revitalize and invigorate, the stimulating peppermint oil will make your skin tingle with life. For quick identification on those hazy mornings, poppyseeds are added so that this bar stands out from the crowd along the edge of the bath.

1. Prepare the mold or molds.

2. Blend the water and lye. Set aside and cool to 120°F.

3. Melt the coconut and palm oils. Blend in the olive oil and either heat or cool to 120°F.

4. Once the temperatures match, blend the lye solution into the oils.

5. Stir the mixture until the soap traces, then add the peppermint leaves, the poppyseeds, and the peppermint and tea tree essential oils. Stir thoroughly and pour into the prepared mold or molds.

6. Leave the soap to set for 8 to 12 hours, or until the soap is solid and firm to the touch. Release the soap from the mold or molds and allow to cure for 4 to 6 weeks.

16 ounces tepid water

6.1 ounces lye

18 ounces coconut oil

6 ounces palm oil

16 ounces olive oil

2 tablespoons finely crushed dried peppermint leaves

1 tablespoon poppyseeds

1 ounce peppermint essential oil

1 ounce tea tree essential oil

Discovered by Australian Aborigines, the healing powers of the tea tree are legendary. In fact, clinical studies have shown it to be one hundred times more powerful than other antiseptics. The essential oil, which is distilled from the leaves and twigs of the tree, is strongly antifungal, antiviral, and antibiotic. Tea tree essential oil is especially wonderful with skin problems and has been used to treat cold sores, warts, acne, burns, candida, athlete's foot, and more—the list just goes on and on.

emu oil & wintergreen
achy-days soap

This soap is a magical blend of an old favorite, wintergreen, and the newly discovered emu oil. When you bathe with this soap, allow the lather to stay on your skin a little longer than usual— so the pain-relieving qualities of emu oil and wintergreen essential oil can penetrate and ease away aches and pains, and tiredness in your joints and muscles.

1. Prepare the mold or molds.

2. Blend the water and lye. Set aside and cool to 150°F.

3. Melt the coconut oil and beeswax. Blend in the olive, castor, and emu oils and either heat or cool to 150°F.

4. Once the temperatures match, blend the lye solution into the oils.

5. Stir the mixture until the soap traces, then add the wintergreen and clary sage essential oils. Stir thoroughly and pour into the prepared mold or molds.

6. Leave the soap to set for 18 to 24 hours, or until the soap is solid and firm to the touch. Release the soap from the mold or molds and allow to cure for 4 to 6 weeks.

14 ounces tepid water

5.8 ounces lye

14 ounces coconut oil

6 ounces beeswax

12 ounces olive oil

6 ounces castor oil

2 ounces emu oil

2 ounces wintergreen essential oil

0.5 ounce clary sage essential oil

wintergreen & emu oil

Wintergreen contains a substance that is molecularly similar to the pain-relieving constituent of aspirin, and has much the same effect. The essential oil is therefore effective for relieving aches and pains— particularly those associated with sore muscles and arthritis. Meanwhile, emu oil is the subject of world wide scientific testing. Researchers have shown that it is of major significance in the treatment of burns—partly because of its anti-inflammatory effect on skin tissue, but also because it reduces scarring. Emu oil is also helpful in the relief of sports-type injuries.

herb-infused oils

Another way to soothe away aches and pains is to use an herb-infused oil for massage. Herb-infused oils take a while to make, but the end result is well worth the effort. Not only do they soothe and relax, but they also bring the herb's individual qualities to bear since herbal oils contain all the properties of the herb from which they are made. This recipe uses calendula, so the oil is very good for healing minor wounds and skin abrasions, but you can substitute other herbs in the same proportions.

1. Place the calendula into a stainless-steel pot and cover with the olive oil. Over medium heat, bring to 100°F. Remove from the heat, cover, and leave to steep.

6 ounces dried calendula flowers

2 pints extra-virgin olive oil

2. For 2 weeks, repeat this procedure twice daily—in the morning and again in the evening.

3. After 2 weeks, prepare your container—you will need one 2-pint jar with a tightly fitting lid. Strain the oil through a fine-mesh filter. Once the oil is strained, it's ready to use. It will keep indefinitely if the jar is kept tightly sealed.

Herb-infused oils make excellent additions to soaps—enriching and adding extra emollience, as well as contributing the herbs' qualities. Calendula-infused oil is included in the Calendula and Cornmeal Exfoliating Bar (see page 46), for example, and comfrey-infused oil is used to make Comfrey and Lavender Shaving Soap (see page 49). Chickweed-and-plantain-infused oil goes on to make Green Herbs Baby Soap (see page 63)—where two herbs are infused together, as here, use equal quantities (3 ounces) of each herb—while chamomile-infused oil is used in Chamomile and Cornmeal Soap (see page 54).

double-mint castille bar

The cooling, refreshing effect of this soap makes it wonderful for showering away the tensions of a long, hot, tiring day. The mints will leave you smelling clean but not perfumed, and feeling revitalized and invigorated. Since this is a Castille-type soap, this recipe may take a little longer than usual to trace.

1. Prepare the mold or molds.

2. Blend the water and lye. Set aside and cool to 110°F.

3. Melt the coconut and palm oils. Blend in the olive oil and either heat or cool to 110°F.

4. Once the temperatures match, blend the lye solution into the oils.

5. Stir the mixture until the soap traces, then add the peppermint and spearmint essential oils. Stir thoroughly and pour into the prepared mold or molds.

6. Leave the soap to set for 24 to 36 hours, or until the soap is solid and firm to the touch. Release the soap from the mold or molds and allow to cure for 6 to 8 weeks.

14.5 ounces tepid water

15.9 ounces lye

8 ounces coconut oil

4 ounces palm oil

28 ounces olive oil

1 ounce peppermint essential oil

1 ounce spearmint essential oil

Apart from being common food flavorings, peppermint and spearmint are natural antiseptics and have a very stimulating nature. Both essential oils are used to treat headaches, nausea, indigestion, and fatigue. The plants thrive in any garden. It is so prolific in fact, it is often considered invasive; so check with your friends and relatives—you'll probably find someone who would be glad to give some away—if you don't have too much yourself, that is.

soapwort shampoo

Introducing a very special ingredient—soapwort—which is combined with rosemary to make this excellent shampoo. Rosemary is chosen for its ability to deep-clean follicles and promote strong, healthy hair. The herb has been proven to encourage hair growth, and is of tremendous value to the scalp—treating dandruff, itchy scalp conditions, and premature balding. If you like, you can adapt the recipe and use any other herb—lavender, for example, would be a good choice. Soapwort does not produce much lather, so use two cups shampoo each time you wash your hair.

32 ounces distilled water

4 tablespoons chopped dried soapwort root

1 tablespoon dried rosemary leaves

1. Prepare the containers—you will need two 16-ounce bottles.

2. Combine the water and soapwort in a saucepan. Cover and bring to a boil. Reduce the heat and simmer for 25 minutes, keeping the pan covered.

3. Remove the pan from the heat and add the rosemary. Replace the lid and leave to cool completely.

4. Strain the shampoo through a fine-mesh strainer and pour into the prepared containers. Use within 5 days and discard any leftovers.

Soapwort is probably the oldest cleansing agent known to man. Also called Bouncing Betty, Sweet Betty, and Wild Sweet William, soapwort has natural cleansing properties because it contains a mildly lathering substance called saponin. When the dried roots of the plant are simmered in water, the saponin cooks out to create a milky, foaming effect. Soapwort is available from bulk herb suppliers and good health food stores.

herbal hair rinses

After using any of the shampoos or soaps in this book, try rinsing with one of these lovely herbal rinses. For healthy, shiny hair, pour the rinse over your hair once you've washed out the lather, leave for a few minutes, and then wash out.

one This simple rosemary tea is good for all hair types. To make, pour the boiling water over the rosemary and steep for 15 minutes. Strain and allow to cool before using the whole recipe on your hair.

64 ounces boiling water

4 ounces fresh rosemary leaves

two Also good for all hair types, this rinse will keep indefinitely if stored in an airtight jar. To make, fill a 32-ounce jar, with a tightly fitting lid, half full with the herbs. Add the vinegar and seal tightly. Shake the jar every day for 2 weeks, then strain. The rinse is ready to use: dilute half a cup rinse in 32 ounces water.

Any combination of the following fresh herbs: rosemary, sage, chamomile, yarrow, basil, lavender, horsetail, and nettle

Apple-cider vinegar

three This rinse is wonderful for both dry and fair hair types. The recipe will make enough to fill two 16-ounce bottles and will keep for up to 7 days in the refrigerator. To make, place the petals, bark, and water in a medium-size saucepan and bring to a boil. Remove from the heat; leave to steep until cool. Strain, add the vinegar, and pour into the containers. To use, dilute half a cup in 32 ounces water.

1 cup calendula petals

0.5 cup white oak bark

24 ounces water

8 ounces apple-cider vinegar

four This rinse is excellent for dark and dull hair types. It will also keep for up to 7 days in the refrigerator. Set out three 12-ounce bottles. To make, place the herbs and water in a medium-size saucepan and bring to a boil. Remove from the heat and leave to steep until cool. Strain, add the vinegar and lemon juice, and pour into the bottles. The rinse is ready to use straightaway. To use, dilute half a cup in 32 ounces water.

4 ounces fresh rosemary

2 ounces fresh elder flowers

2 ounces fresh nettles

1 ounce fresh horsetail leaves

1 ounce dried walnut leaves, ground

32 ounces water

8 ounces apple-cider vinegar

2 tablespoons lemon juice

herbal bath bags

These little muslin bags, filled with combinations of dried herbs and flowers, are a delight. Throw one under the running water as the bath fills for a heavenly bathing experience—you can also use the bag as a washcloth. Apart from the herb blends, the bags also include soapwort and oatmeal, for their gentle cleansing and antiseptic properties. The muslin bags themselves are very simple to make, but they are also readily available at garden and craft stores, and through catalogs.

1. Prepare the bags—the following blends will yield sufficient mix to fill ten 2- x 3-inch drawstring bags.

2. In a bowl, mix together the ingredients for your chosen blend.

3. Spoon the mixture into the bags, and pull up and tie the drawstring.

rosemary & lavender blend

4 ounces rolled oats, chopped

2 ounces lavender leaves, chopped

2 ounces rosemary leaves, chopped

1 ounce soapwort powder

spearmint & elder flower blend

4 ounces rolled oats, chopped

2 ounces elder flowers, crushed

2 ounces nettle leaves, crushed

2 ounces spearmint, crushed

1 ounce soapwort powder

sweet summer blend

4 ounces rolled oats, chopped

2 ounces lavender leaves and flowers, chopped

2 ounces rose petals

1 ounce dried lovage root, chopped

1 ounce soapwort power

lemon

lavender shower gel

This is another recipe where soapwort is the star. Although this refreshing, lavender-scented shower gel won't lather, it will gently cleanse and moisturize, leaving your skin feeling clean, soft, and smooth.

1. In a food processor, process one cup of the lavender with the Everclear, until the lavender is finely chopped. Pour the mixture into a jar, seal tightly, and leave to sit for 24 hours; strain.

2. Bring the distilled water to a boil and add the soapwort. Simmer for 15 minutes, then remove the pan from the heat, and add the remaining one cup of lavender. Cover and allow to steep for 8 to 12 hours; strain.

3. Prepare the containers—you will need eight wide-mouthed 4-ounce jars with tightly fitting lids

4. Combine the lavender-alcohol extract and the soapwort mixture in a medium-size saucepan and bring to a boil. Whisk in the arrowroot and simmer, stirring continuously, until the mixture thickens and becomes clear.

5. Stir in the lavender essential oil and pour into the prepared containers.

2 cups chopped dried lavender leaves and flowers

2 ounces Everclear or grain alcohol

32 ounces distilled water

3 ounces chopped or powdered soapwort

0.25 cup arrowroot powder

1 ounce lavender essential oil

silky-smooth herbal bath oil

This sweetly scented bath oil makes the water and your skin feel silky smooth and wonderful. The blend of eucalyptus, lavender, and geranium essential oils provides a delicious aroma, while the castor, jojoba, almond, and safflower oils moisturize your skin—leaving it soft and supple. Add two or three tablespoons to your bath as it fills and enjoy a long, relaxing soak.

1. Prepare the container—you will need one 16-ounce bottle.

2. In a bowl, mix all of the ingredients together and pour into the prepared container. Leave to stand for 4 days, to allow the oils to blend, then start running your bath.

8 ounces safflower oil

4 ounces castor oil

2 ounces jojoba oil

2 ounces sweet almond oil

30 drops eucalyptus essential oil

30 drops lavender essential oil

10 drops geranium essential oil

safflower & sweet almond oils

Safflower and sweet almond oils are most frequently used as "carriers" for essential oils. Because most essential oils are toxic if applied directly to the skin, they need to be diluted in carrier oils before they can be safely added to baths, used for massage, and so on. Safflower oil disperses well in water, a useful quality for a carrier oil, and is a good source of vitamin E. Sweet almond oil is an excellent all-purpose bath-and-massage oil because it is very moisturizing and emollient. Safflower oil is available in grocery stores, and both are available in natural food stores—but be sure to buy the pure versions, not blends.

resources

ANGEL'S EARTH
1633 Scheffer Avenue
St. Paul, MN 55116
(612) 698-3601
fax: (612) 698-3636
e-mail: a-earth@concentric.net
**General soap-making supplies,
essential oils**

ARISTA
1082 Post Road
Darien, CT 06820
(800) 255-6457
Castor oil, wheat germ oil

AROMA MEDICA
900 Bethlehem Pike
Erdenheim, PA 19038
(215) 233-5210
fax: (215) 836-0760
Essential oils

BARKER'S ENTERPRISES, INC.
15106 10th Avenue SW
Seattle, WA 98166
(206) 244-1870
Molds, dyes

BRUSHY MOUNTAIN BEE FARM
610 Bethany Church Road
Moravian Falls, NC 28654
(910) 921-3640 and
(800) 233-7929
fax: (910) 921-2681
**Beeswax, molds, glycerin
soap base, dyes**

**CALIFORNIA OLIVE OIL
MANUFACTURING COMPANY**
PO Box 247
1301 I Street
Reedley, CA 93654
(209) 638-2231
Olive oil

CHEMICALS, INC.
270 Osborne Drive
Fairfield, OH 45014
(513) 682-2000
Lye (50 pound minimum)

CHEM LAB SUPPLIES
1060 Ortega Way, Unit C
Placentia, CA 92670
(714) 630-7902
fax: (714) 630-3553
Lye, electronic scales

**CONSOLIDATED PLASTICS
COMPANY, INC.**
8181 Darrow Road
Twinsburg, OH 44087
(800) 362-1000
fax: (216) 425-3333
Spatulas, thermometers, scales

CREATION HERBAL PRODUCTS
PO Box 344
10492 US Highway 421
Deep Gap, NC 28618
(704) 262-0006
fax: (704) 262-1178
e-mail: creationsoap@boone.net
http://www.creationherbal.com
**Wheat Germ, castor, coconut,
and palm oils, essential oils,
glycerin soap base, molds,
soap-making kits, herbs,
glycerin, rosewater, beeswax,
herbal extracts and infused oils**

DADANT & SONS, INC.
136 Route 17C
Waverly, NY 14892
(717) 465-3232
Beeswax

DEMARLE
2666-B Route 130 North
Cranbury, NJ 08512
(609) 395-0219
Molds

DESERT BALM
PO Box 659
Avila Beach, CA 93424
(800) 729-2256
Jojoba oil

EAST END IMPORT COMPANY
PO Box 107
47 North Shore Road
Montauk, NY 11954
(516) 668-4158
Essential oils, floral water

FUJI VEGETABLE OIL, INC.
1 Barker Avenue, Suite 290
White Plains, NY 10601
(914) 761-7900
Palm oil, coconut oil

**GARDEN OF FRAGRANCES AND
AROMATICS**
141 Court Street
Brooklyn, NY 11201
(718) 625-6340
fax: (718) 625-6783
Essential oils

GLORYBEE
120 North Seneca
Eugene, OR 97402
(541) 689-0913 and
(800) 456-7923
Beeswax

GOOD FOOD
4960 Horseshoe Pike
Honey Brook, PA 19344
(610) 273-3776 and
(800) 327-4406
fax: (610) 273-7652
Olive, coconut, and palm oils

GROVEL'S
PO Box 281
Port Perry, ON L9L 1A3
Canada
(905) 985-0079 and
(905) 985-4788
**Essential oils, jojoba, and
sweet almond oil**

**HARLAN FAIRBANKS
COMPANY, LTD**
12031 No. 5 Road
Richmond, BC V7A 4E9
Canada
(604) 275-8445
Coconut oil

JANCA
456 East Juanita #7
Mesa, AR 85204
(602) 497-9494
Vegetable and essential oils

LAVENDER LANE
7337 #1 Roseville Road
Sacramento, CA 95842
(916) 334-4400
Oils, bottles, jars

LORANN OILS
PO Box 22009
4518 Aurelius Road
Lansing, MI 48909
(800) 248-1302
Essential oils

L V LOMAS
99 Summerlea Road
Brampton, ON L6T 4V2
Canada
(905) 458-7111 and
(416) 417-1097
Oils, essential oils

LYE CHEMICAL SERVICES
2600 Thunderhawk Court
Dayton, OH 45414
(800) 576-2436
Lye (50 pound minimum)

MIDATLANTIC
193 Christie Street
Newark, NJ 07105
(201) 465-0747
Oils

MID-CON
1465 North Winchester
Olathe, KS 66061
(800) 547-1392
**Bottles and jars, molds,
scents, dyes**

**MILLENIUM NATURAL
PRODUCTS CORPORATION**
Route 2, Box 2503
Alto, TX 75925
(888) 244-9578
Essential oils

**MISSOURI CANDLE &
WAX COMPANY**
707 Park Avenue
St. Louis, MO 63104
(314) 241-3544 and
(800) 894-8531
Beeswax, molds

NEFERTUM AROMATICS
45 Navy St. #A
Venice, CA 90291
(818) 754-0087 and
(800) 731-4950
fax: (818) 508-0009
Essential oils

POURETTE
1418 Northwest 53rd St.
Seattle, WA 98107
(800) 888-9425
**General supplies for
making glycerin soaps**

PURE PRO OILS, INC.
955 Massachusetts Avenue,
Suite 232
Cambridge, MA 02139
(800) 900-7873
**Essential oils, sweet almond
and safflower oils**

ROBERTET, INC.
PO Box 650
125 Bauer Drive
Oakland, NJ 07436-3190
(201) 337-7100
Essential oils

SCENTS OF HARMONY
PO Box 28082
13111 West Alameda Parkway #16
Lakewood, CO 80228
(303) 716-1037
Essential oils

THE BOSTON JOJOBA COMPANY
PO Box 771
Middleton, MA 01949
(800) 256-5622
fax: (508) 777-9332
Jojoba oil

index

Entries and page numbers in bold refer to individual recipes.
Page numbers in italics refer to photographs.

Acknowledgments

The author would like to thank:

Anna Carter, for teaching him
how to make soap and for
helping to develop the
recipes in this book; and

Brushy Mountain Bee Farm,
for the seashell melt-and-pour soaps pictured; and

Melinda Novack of Sag Harbor Soap Company
for some of the cold-process soaps pictured.